T0285729

BOLD
KINDNESS

BOLD
KINDNESS

A CARING, MORE COMPASSIONATE
WAY TO LEAD

CATHY
THORPE

FAST
COMPANY
Press

Fast Company Press
New York, New York
www.fastcompanypress.com

Distributed by Greenleaf Book Group

For ordering information or special discounts for bulk purchases, please contact Greenleaf Book Group at PO Box 91869, Austin, TX 78709, 512.891.6100.

Design and composition by Greenleaf Book Group
Cover design by Greenleaf Book Group and Hannah Gaskamp
Cover image used under license from ©Shutterstock/Gisele Yashar and ©Shutterstock/world of vector

Publisher's Cataloging-in-Publication data is available.

Print ISBN: 978-1-63908-053-3

eBook ISBN: 978-1-63908-054-0

To offset the number of trees consumed in the printing of our books, Greenleaf donates a portion of the proceeds from each printing to the Arbor Day Foundation. Greenleaf Book Group has replaced over 50,000 trees since 2007.

Printed in the United States of America on acid-free paper

23 24 25 26 27 28 29 30   10 9 8 7 6 5 4 3 2 1

First Edition

This book is dedicated to you: a person who is curious about how you can challenge and improve traditional business practices and who wants to discover a bolder, kinder approach to developing people. Thank you for joining me on this journey.

CONTENTS

Introduction: A Better Way of Doing Business. 1

PART ONE: Bold Kind Workplace 7

Chapter 1: The Drive to Do Better 9

Chapter 2: From Bold to Bold Kindness:
the Nurse Next Door Journey. 19

Chapter 3: The Business of Bold Kindness 31

PART TWO: Bold Kind Self 45

Chapter 4: Showing Up as a Fully Expressed Self 49

Chapter 5: Unconventional Skills to Fuel
Bold Kind Leadership 65

Chapter 6: Leadership Commitments of
a Bold Kind Leader. 81

PART THREE: Bold Kind Culture 93

Chapter 7: A Caring Foundation 99

Chapter 8: Cultivating Self-Led Leaders 119

Chapter 9: Abundance Mindset 133

Chapter 10: REAL Conversations 151

Chapter 11: Mentoring, Not Managing 165

Epilogue: Bold Kindness Never Stops 181

Acknowledgments 185

About Me. 187

A BETTER WAY OF DOING BUSINESS

I magine a workplace where people can be *themselves*. Their true, authentic selves—whether they're funny or serious, quiet or outgoing. Where people can be honest with their colleagues and say what needs to be said, without worrying about stepping on toes or thinking they may be asking stupid questions. Where they aren't afraid they're going to get fired if they disagree with their boss. Where there aren't hierarchies or power dynamics.

Imagine an environment in which people support each other and candidly share ideas and opportunities without trying to protect their jobs or make someone else look bad. A team without egos. Team members who continuously find ways to better themselves and their work because it makes them feel excited and fulfilled. Where they feel they can show excitement when they're happy or express sadness about something that has happened in their personal life and need a minute to reflect.

And imagine if, instead of a small group of top executives calling the shots, *every team member* has a place at the table and contributions from everyone are welcome. Where all team members are fully responsible for the decisions they make because they care deeply about their work and take accountability for those decisions.

Now, imagine you could achieve these goals all while making your business stronger and better. Some people might think that's far-fetched. I disagree.

I've worked in traditional business environments where the expectation is to follow orders, wait to be told what to do and not question why. I have firsthand experience working in business environments where I either felt I had to or was actually told to hide parts of my true self while at work. I've seen what happens when people's contributions are diminished and creativity is discouraged. And frankly, it's demoralizing. It creates workplaces in which people aren't inspired; they simply do whatever it takes to get through the day.

I've also experienced a better way of leading, which I'm truly excited about. Since I joined Nurse Next Door, an organization that provides in-home care for seniors, my leadership team and I have been shunning traditional business practices and using a new way to lead others and grow our business. This approach is what we call Bold Kindness. It's the term we use to describe a workplace free of ego and hierarchy, where teams are engaged, self-led and love coming to work—all while focusing on creating an energized, productive, creative business.

Bold Kindness is a culture and leadership philosophy that

reflects a kinder, more compassionate way of developing people. It challenges traditional business practices by promoting a new approach to organizational culture and leadership practices. It's how we show up in our personal and professional lives and, just as importantly, how we interact with our people, caregivers, and clients.

This is how Bold Kindness shows up at Nurse Next Door:

- There is strong energy and excitement that come from thinking disruptively and pursuing a mission that provides focus and purpose.

- We give our team and clients more choice in their lives to help them be successful no matter which direction they choose.

- People are able to contribute more fully in the workplace and be more present in all aspects of their lives.

- We are able to be vulnerable and have honest, meaningful conversations with people about how we can do better and be better.

- We have all developed closer connections with the things that give our lives meaning.

- Our leaders act as mentors and guides rather than bosses.

Best of all? Embracing these concepts is not an *outcome* of having a strong business; they are the *ingredients*, the inputs, required to become stronger and more successful. In the last seven years, we've generated 20–30 percent year-over-year growth. We have secured industry-first partnerships, including a partnership with a major hospital system in California. We tripled the size of the company, expanding globally from the original three Canadian franchises in 2007 to hundreds of franchises across Canada, the US, Australia and England. Our client and caregiver Net Promoter Scores (NPS) have risen dramatically; as of 2022, it was 67 for clients and 74 for caregivers. (In health care, the average 2022 client NPS score was 38.)

For us at Nurse Next Door, having a culture of Bold Kindness *works*. It's transforming our company. Our team members are genuinely excited to come to work and are surrounded by projects and people that excite them. Our team feels valued, respected and empowered. Equally important, they get to live ONE life and have one version of themselves that integrates the professional and personal. They get to come to work showing up as their fully expressed selves. It really comes down to creating an environment that truly engages people and challenges them to do their very best.

Bold Kindness Can Work for You

Bold Kindness is transforming Nurse Next Door's industry: We're setting a new standard for home care. I believe Bold Kindness can work for *any* industry, not just home care. And that's why I decided to write this book: to describe the culture and leadership philosophy that my team and I have used at Nurse Next Door to create an engaged and inspiring workplace.

My hope is for this book to inspire you to reflect on your

own leadership and organization, challenge traditional ways of doing business and explore how Bold Kindness can help inspire a culture of people development.

The book is composed of three sections:

Part 1: Bold Kind Workplace is about why we need Bold Kindness in our organizations and the course corrections that have taken Nurse Next Door in that direction.

Part 2: Bold Kind Self addresses the things Nurse Next Door has done to develop and fully express ourselves. I really believe that the only way we can support other people in their journey is by getting curious and examining our own attitudes and leadership approaches.

At Nurse Next Door, this work is never done. In my quest to be a Bold Kind leader, I've had to take a good, honest look at myself. I've had to be really curious and vulnerable about who I am and go to uncomfortable places to find the best version of myself. I've had to learn to be really humble. And you know, some days I'm more patient than others; some days I lean into feedback more than other days. And I have to be okay with that. I'm always learning and growing. I don't have to be an expert at everything I do. I just have to be willing to put myself out there.

Part 3: Bold Kind Culture describes the specific practices we've used at Nurse Next Door for developing people and creating an engaging workplace, which is something we've done an amazing job of. It's about how we take someone who starts in our Care Services Center (our call center) and help build their career. It's about how we ensure our people are happy to come to work and aren't longing for Friday to come.

Throughout this book, you'll find Bold Kind reflection questions you can use to stimulate your thinking about how you and your organization can move in a Bold Kind direction. They are based on questions I originally created just for myself, which I go back to on a regular basis to see how I'm doing and to continue to challenge myself in my growth. People have told me how useful they found them, so I've included them here. You may find them to be helpful entryways for exploring each chapter topic.

I firmly believe that we, as a society and as business leaders, have an amazing opportunity to get back to the authenticity of our experience: the simplicity of showing up as a person and ensuring others thrive in their lives and work so they're not living in fear. After all, who wants to live an ordinary life where we're doing things we *think* we should do? Why not take a chance, do something differently and make life and work extraordinary?

It begins with a conversation around new ideas.

So, let's get it started.

PART ONE

BOLD KIND
WORKPLACE

believe we've spent a long time making business be something that people have to endure, with ineffective workplace cultures that force us to be what we're not. People aren't driven to do and be their best. According to Gallup,[1] only 20 percent of people are engaged at work. And while we've seen small shifts over the years—particularly with more progressive companies that are starting to see the importance of an engaged workforce—there is still so much to be done.

My experience at Nurse Next Door has shown me that we can do better. A lot better. In the following sections, I want to show you the possibility of what can happen when leaders and organizations embrace Bold Kindness. I get into why we should challenge the traditional leadership mindset. Then I talk about how Bold Kindness is helping Nurse Next Door make lives better and create a more caring organization. I also demonstrate how Nurse Next Door is accelerating our growth by prioritizing people and incorporating unconventional cultural practices on a daily basis.

Is this work easy? Definitely not. Will you make mistakes if you incorporate some of the concepts? Undoubtedly. And that's okay! This work has the potential to be truly transformative.

---

1   "State of the Global Workspace: 2022 Report," Gallup, accessed October 2022, https://www.gallup.com/workplace/349484/state-of-the-global-workplace.aspx.

Chapter 1

THE DRIVE TO DO BETTER

This book arose in part from my journey in being a mom. When my kids were young, I saw the impact that parenting styles—including language and actions—have on children. And as I got curious about that, I also started to see how leadership styles affect our businesses in many ways.

We have all been groomed from a young age to function in formal, rigid systems. This starts when we are in school and extends into our adult lives, including our business careers. I look at my kids going through the motions of learning in structured, archaic educational institutions. Their experiences at school are, in essence, identical to mine. They're being prepared to be compliant, just like I was. Challenging the norm is often considered a problem.

I was primed to respond to exam questions just like my peers, to choose a focus area from a limited pool of courses and, upon graduation, to enter a workforce where I was hired simply because I aligned with a predetermined set of requirements. It says a lot that not much has changed in the thirty years since I was in my kids' shoes.

I don't want a world in which my kids have to make personal sacrifices just to align with someone else's vision of what they want their business to look like. A Bold Kind workplace is the type of workplace I want to see for my kids: a place where we've dropped the cubicle walls and opened up the organization. Where people can be real, empowered, connected and cared for, and want to come into work every day.

To create a new kind of organization, we have to develop a new vision of leadership, which is what I explore in this chapter.

Challenging the Norm

The workplace has long been a formal environment in which a team member is seen as one side of a transactional relationship, where they are expected to leave their home life at home and bring their work life home.

Sometimes this happens in a subtle way, and sometimes it's obvious. They might make a small mistake and worry all day about potential repercussions. Or talk too much in a meeting. Or say the wrong thing. Or keep their mouth shut when they don't think something is working, then go home and complain to their spouse about it. I had a team member once tell me that at their former place of employment, they were told to stop being so outgoing. This person went to work every day trying to rein it in. She was so exhausted trying to be something she wasn't that she quit her job after three months.

There's a hierarchy in organizations in terms of what's appropriate and what's not. People do the work, and at the end of the day, they're relieved to be getting a break for the evening. And then they start all over again the next day.

I once worked for a company that frowned on people taking off time if their child was sick. We were simply expected to find childcare. I had to take off my "mom hat" before I entered the office and put it back on when I left. It was mentally exhausting. I felt like I had become a chameleon—a reflection of my surroundings—changing how I behaved depending on where I was. Being ourselves at work—and bringing our roles as mom, dad, husband, wife, sister, brother or friend into the office—has typically come at a price.

Over the years, I've done what it took to climb up the ladder. I've done what I thought was needed to make it in the business world. I was careful: I knew if I was too assertive or voiced my boundaries and expectations, people might think I was being difficult. If I was kind, I might be seen as weak. I had to camouflage my true self to fit the business mold, and I was shut down if I broke character.

Fortunately, I eventually came to see that I could be a much more effective leader if I was brave enough to show the real me.

Developing a Personal Leadership Style

In the 1990s, I joined a global retail organization and had the opportunity to dive into a variety of operational initiatives, including leading a team in Germany, expanding the company brand, and helping place them on the global retail map. At that time, many US businesses were moving forward with expansion "firsts." For me, this was also my first experience treading into an international retail market, and it was really scary at times. We went through a lot of changes and challenges. I learned, very quickly, that those challenges are best overcome when you have a strong team guided by confident and passionate leaders. And along the way, I met people, got curious and learned things that eventually gave me the courage to develop my own leadership style.

I particularly remember one leader I had while I was with this organization. He came out to visit me while I was overseeing our Germany flagship location. He completely stood out from anybody else because he listened to me and encouraged me to contribute. He wanted me to succeed, and he invested in me. What's more, he encouraged me to be *me* and never tried to mold me into something I wasn't.

I considered him more of a mentor than a leader (a theme you'll see throughout this book) because he helped me grow and make my own choices, instead of telling me what to do or dictating what direction I should take. We might spend the morning diving into business—reviewing processes and making business decisions to improve results—then in the afternoon we'd drive to a meeting, zooming along the autobahn, singing at the top of our lungs to a song we loved and having a great time. I never had to be a different version of myself when I was with him. He was always 100 percent himself and fully expressed.

That experience and relationship had a profound effect on me because I realized I could be at work and be *me* at the same time. I had never felt that before.

And it grew from there. I saw possibilities. I started asking questions. I saw versions of myself that I didn't want to be. I began integrating elements of what I learned into various jobs and into my consulting work.

REMOVING FEAR FROM BUSINESS

Fear has historically been a big part of business culture. The fear of being ourselves and being judged by our colleagues. The fear of making a mistake. Of upsetting a boss. The fear of being fired. As a result of fear, too many people stifle their true selves and are afraid to make a genuine contribution.

I believe it's time we remove fear from organizations. When we go to work without fear, we bring our best, most authentic selves. We speak up when we disagree, whether we're with a colleague or a leader. We're not afraid to be silly. We have genuine, open conversations about challenges. We bring the good, the bad, the raw and the real. We are able to truly express ourselves. The personal and professional blend into one. When we work without fear, we are not afraid to take chances on a new project, even if we make mistakes.

It's time to work like we are not afraid to get fired. It's time to work with authenticity and confidence.

Finding a Different Way

A lot of the problems with traditional workplaces really came to light when the pandemic hit. Businesses had to transform overnight—restructuring, laying people off, finding new business models—and their people followed suit. Suddenly people started questioning the value of their lives at work and began reassessing what was important to them. They were no longer willing to put up with workplaces that valued profits over people. The unexpected benefit of the pandemic is that it has given us a chance to question and challenge ourselves, both personally and professionally.

And here's the really interesting thing to me. Now that so many people have started to make shifts in how they live their lives and conduct their business, many of them aren't going back to the way they were before. They want something more. It's an exciting opportunity for all of us.

I think of it in terms of nature, like an earthquake. An earthquake occurs. The tectonic plates in the earth shift, and the landscape changes in some way. A mountain rises, or an island starts forming. And once the land changes, it can't go back to the way it was.

The same thing is happening with business. A fundamental shift in business is happening, and we can't go back to the way it was. There is a real desire to change how we interact as people, in both our personal and professional lives. It is all *one* life! We have the opportunity to bring humanity to business and how we work: to a new, more personal level that sheds hierarchies, focuses on the growth and development of team members and, most importantly, cares for people.

Even as the pandemic has continued to get more under control, this fundamental change, this disruption in business, isn't going to go away. I don't believe it *should* go away. Companies have learned too much. People have reevaluated their values and priorities in life. They see they can adapt more quickly than they thought and transform their businesses in ways they hadn't dreamed of. Business as usual doesn't cut it anymore. To be profitable and grow, businesses need to put their team members first. The world has changed. What's seen can't be unseen. We can take back control of our lives, dreams and workplaces, and make the impossible happen.

Since the pandemic, I've seen people quitting their jobs in droves. And I believe it's because they are no longer willing to accept the traditional ways of doing business: the top-down hierarchy, the bosses who are feared, the mindset of command and control. The requirement to change business leadership is here. People want things that matter. They want relationships, not transactions. To be heard and listened to. To have bosses who care about them and coworkers who treat them with respect. People want more authenticity and vulnerability in the workplace.

I know that changing leadership and people practices can feel daunting. We can feel alone in the process, especially if we're with organizations that seem to be locked in the past. And this is particularly true for women and marginalized communities, who are traditionally far more challenged when it comes to being heard in the workplace and effecting change.

Becoming a Bold Kind Leader

In 2021, a significant life event happened that altered my world. My husband passed away, and everything changed. We had been married for over twenty years, and he supported me unconditionally. He was an incredible father and centered his world around his family. To those who knew my husband, they experienced one of the most generous, passionate and humorous men they had ever met. His laughter was contagious and ignited a room. In addition to being an amazing and worldly human being, he was also my cheerleader. He played an important role in helping me challenge myself and be true to my own personal leadership approach.

Since that time, I have continued to be inspired to take a good look at my world and my life and how I want to disrupt it. I am investing in reinventing who I am, and I know my husband would be very proud. I think this is pretty important to share because it's part of my journey to be a Bold Kind leader.

As part of that journey, I've realized that for me, there is no leadership persona. I don't believe leadership should be a power-oriented, hierarchical thing. For me, it's having the confidence in knowing I treat people really well, and that I work on kindness and self-discipline every day. It's that inner work. I think that's what transforms leadership. It's really just us continually working on ourselves as people. It's as much about leading people at work as it is leading our lives or being a great mom or partner.

The work of Bold Kind leadership is also about being curious and humble. And if that work doesn't come from a place of kindness, it's not going to work. For me, it's not about dictating the way for people to move forward. It's simply sharing a vision of what's possible. I want to be in a different conversation about how people are led and how they feel about their work, their roles and ultimately their lives.

As part of my journey to be a Bold Kind leader, I have realized that I need to take Bold Kindness to a new level: to get crystal clear on its principles and start sharing them with the world. In my heart, I know I want to disrupt the business community and help get the conversation started about how we can transform business.

I would like to encourage other leaders to start taking a good, long look at the workplaces we're in. We should be asking ourselves questions. *When do we get to bring our full selves to work and be the best versions of ourselves that we can be? When do we get to be empowered at work and be given the space we need to do our jobs (and do them well) without fear?*

As leaders, are we enabling our teams to live and work at their highest potential? Is our current organizational model serving us or hindering us? Is it possible there's a different, better way? Are people living and working at their highest level? How do we feel when Monday comes? Are we excited to be going back to work, or resigned to it?

We have one life, and time is finite. Let's spend that time being our true selves.

CHAPTER 2

FROM BOLD TO BOLD KINDNESS: THE NURSE NEXT DOOR JOURNEY

Nurse Next Door started in 2001 as a small, founder-led business in Vancouver, British Columbia, Canada. When our founders Ken Sim and John DeHart decided to move into the home health care space, they knew the industry was tired and old, with models of care that hadn't changed in decades. They didn't want to open just another home care company; they wanted to find a better way of providing care. They wanted to be bold. They wanted to be disruptive. And those goals pertained to both the services the company would provide and the way it would be run.

Nurse Next Door has since grown from a single business to a franchise operation with over two hundred fifty locations across North America and a master franchise in Australia and England. We are pursuing our global ambitions and expanding into additional countries. I share the details of Nurse Next Door's evolution into a Bold Kind organization throughout this book and am providing an overview first so you can see how all the pieces fit together.

Our Purpose: Making Lives Better

When they decided to start Nurse Next Door, founders Ken and John asked themselves, *How can we find a better way of providing home care?*

One thing they knew was that people overwhelmingly want to stay at home as they age rather than spend their final days or years in a nursing home.[2] Home is where people feel comfortable, and it's where they want to be.

A lot of people don't know that aging at home is an option. The norm has been for people to go to a retirement home, and we want to be the voice to shift that conversation. We want to be the ones saying, "Yes, you can stay at home," when so many others are saying, "No, home isn't the place to be." We have a strong belief in what we are doing and an unapologetic point of view.

In our radio ads, we openly speak a blunt truth that few people *want* to move into a retirement home. By articulating this, we're not trying to make people comfortable. We want to be

---

2   March of Dimes Canada, "National Survey Shows Canadians Overwhelmingly Want to Age at Home; Just One-Quarter of Seniors Expect to Do So," April 27, 2021, https://www.newswire.ca/news-releases/national-survey-shows-canadians -overwhelmingly-want-to-age-at-home-just-one-quarter-of-seniors-expect-to -do-so-842023628.html.

sure our advertising sparks a conversation and makes a distinct impression as a brand. We also want to bring to the forefront necessary conversations that people may be afraid to have or don't want to have. The thing is, those conversations are *hard*. And hard conversations are the most important.

Once they decided on providing in-home care, Ken and John knew it would be critical to support clients' physical needs and ensure they are safe and taken care of. That's why the core of Nurse Next Door's services revolve around a range of medical and nonmedical services to help clients, whether they have a chronic illness or simply need help with daily activities.

Because the health and safety of our clients—and our caregivers—is top of mind, we are very intentional about our interactions and decisions. We ensure we are using and enforcing correct protocols and making deliberate choices that reflect safety, care and wellness. Paying attention to processes and standards is key.

However, while it's essential to support *physical* needs, Ken and John also wanted to support people's *whole* needs. Our teams pay attention to seniors' mental and emotional wellness and help them find moments of joy by delivering on the company's purpose, Making Lives Better.

What is so wonderful about Nurse Next Door is that, as a home care provider, caring for people is what we do. We're caregivers, nurses, companions, team members and franchisees. We not only provide assistance with personal and medical care and help clients and their families with daily tasks, we also help people stay at home and live happier lives.

In short, we have stepped beyond *physical* care and into *humanized* care in which we truly care for our clients and focus on making their lives better. This in itself is a form of disruption. Doing the "normal" thing has never been in our psyche: Nurse Next Door's entire goal is around completely disrupting the industry we work in!

Our Care Philosophy: Happier Aging

Ultimately, Nurse Next Door wants to change the perceptions of aging. We are continually inspired by Atul Gawande's book *Being Mortal*, in which he passionately addresses the need to enhance our quality of life as we age and to reframe what it means to get older. As he states, "Our ultimate goal, after all, is not a good death but a good life to the very end."[3]

Ken and John asked themselves, *What do people really want? What does it take to make our clients' lives better? What are they looking for?* The answer: people want to be happy. So they decided to disrupt the industry and create a model in which seniors could find joy.

They started with the premise that sadness and helplessness are not inevitable for older adults, even if they are sick or have a terminal illness. People should always be able to find hope and joy, regardless of where they are in life. We believe that life can be fulfilling, regardless of how old someone is or what stage of life they're at.

---

3   Atul Gawande, *Being Mortal* (Picador: New York, 2014).

Because of this thinking, we developed Happier Aging, our care philosophy and the core of our brand. Happier Aging encompasses the following five principles:

1. **Choice:** Doing what we want, when we want, and being able to make decisions for ourselves.

2. **Purpose:** Doing what we love and contributing meaningfully. It's what motivates us to show up for ourselves and others.

3. **Belonging:** Accepting ourselves and others for who we are by cultivating self-worth and self-acceptance and by making community connections.

4. **Respect:** Showing care, concern and consideration for others, even when they are different from us.

5. **Autonomy:** Our right to make decisions for ourselves, free of outside influences, and be the authors of our lives.

Happier Aging is simple yet unconventional. Whenever we meet with a new client, we ask them a question: "What did you used to love doing that you no longer do?" There is a very important reason we ask this question. We want to identify the areas that bring the most happiness to seniors' lives and find ways for them to experience those things. We then do our best to bring that happiness back, acting with boldness and kindness as much as we can.

For instance, one of our caregivers may bring a client flowers for no reason. We might hold a birthday party for someone who is bedridden or take someone to a pool if we find they love swimming. We also look for small ways of helping someone, such as bringing them tea or helping them with gardening.

An incredibly important thing we realized about Happier Aging is that it is a fundamental concept that belongs to *everyone*: ourselves, our clients, our teams, our communities, the world. We all want to be happier as we age, whether we're thirty or ninety. We all want to have meaningful lives, whether we are at home or at work, and to have *choice, purpose, belonging, respect* and *autonomy*.

When we come to work every day at Nurse Next Door, our entire objective is to make lives better for our clients, their families, our fellow team members and everyone we meet. Every single one of us, every single day, including all of our franchisees in North America, England, Australia and beyond, make a deliberate and concerted effort to conscientiously integrate Making Lives Better into our day-to-day interactions. We have found a way to care for our clients, and our teams as well, both personally and professionally, while driving results. It can be as simple as sharing a laugh in the hallway, actively listening to what someone has to say or inviting them to try a new activity. These aren't superficial gestures; these are genuine acts of kindness and caring that come from people with heart.

Evolving Bold Kindness

When I started the interview process to work at Nurse Next Door, I was very attracted to the organization because I saw how my personal philosophy and beliefs could thrive and help the company grow and prosper even more.

The company was already bold when I started here: From the beginning, they had dared to disrupt the status quo in the home care industry. They also had the essence of kindness captured in the Happier Aging philosophy, which I think is really amazing.

With these core elements in place, it was a natural evolution to apply the philosophy across everything we do: how we work with clients and how we care for people in general. By bringing my own perspective into how we run the company, we made Bold Kindness the defining philosophy for Nurse Next Door. It enables everyone who works for us to have the same things we offer our clients: *choice, purpose, belonging, respect* and *autonomy*.

Bold Kindness has evolved over time and is always about caring for others, bringing an Abundance Mindset to the workplace and empowering ourselves and others to be fully expressed. In this way, we're able to live with purpose and choice and find a sense of belonging by respecting and caring for others. We approach our work and our lives from a perspective of abundance, not scarcity.

While it can take years to see culture shift—especially in a radical way—I'm proud of how far we've come since bringing Bold Kindness to Nurse Next Door. I've outlined below some of our accomplishments, which reflect our Bold Kind approach. I think of them as Bold because they are breaking the norms of how business is conducted. I think of them as Kind because they come from a true desire to make someone else's life better.

- We encourage our team to bring their authentic selves to work and fully express who they are. We don't want them to change their persona when they step through our doors.

- We empower our people to dream boldly and help them achieve that dream—even when it is outside of their job description or outside of work.

- We don't dwell on what worked in the past or get stuck in the "if it ain't broke, don't fix it" mentality; we're always trying to do better and improve the future. It is part of our Continuous Improvement Mindset.

- We encourage our team members to be self-led leaders, which means giving everyone—regardless of their experience level or tenure at the company—the power to make decisions.

- We've radically overhauled our organization by removing the middle management hierarchy. Since we have a flat organization, no one worries about speaking candidly or overstepping their position.

- We've internally developed and promoted over 60 percent of our team. We believe in cultivating existing talent, instead of always bringing in outside hires.

- We've done away internally with our leadership team and replaced it with a mentorship team. Rather than having this team tell others what to do, they help support other people in finding solutions.

LEADERS VERSUS MENTORS

In most organizations, the concept of mentorship often reflects a hierarchical approach. An individual will typically decide they need coaching and guidance and reach out to someone they see as an expert or authority figure. Or vice versa: Someone with authority or expertise may offer guidance to a less-experienced colleague or associate. In many cases, the mentor and mentee do not work for the same organization and are therefore not aligned on an organizational chart.

At Nurse Next Door, however, we have a more informal approach. All of our leaders are considered mentors. They serve as trusted advisers and provide direction and guidance to their team members. They don't give orders or act like they are the ultimate authority.

So keep in mind that throughout the rest of this book, when I talk about leaders, I'm really talking about people who mentor and nurture their team and empower them to do their best work. It's an important distinction. It removes the power dynamics and instead empowers team members to be self-led and actively contribute to the business and drive results.

Near the end of the book, I provide a more in-depth look at how we mentor, not manage, at Nurse Next Door.

Welcoming Change

When Nurse Next Door started, the owners knew franchisees personally. The organization had a real family feel, and the business was very successful. However, we had plateaued in terms of financial growth. That's when we knew we needed to shift and start looking at how we could mature and build the company.

We wanted to bring our Bold Kind culture to everyone across the organization, including all franchisees. We also wanted to be very careful about ensuring our culture, purpose and vision of Happier Aging remained the same, while simultaneously bringing our company to the next level.

So we shifted our standard of excellence, where 80 percent was no longer acceptable. We focused on developing team members, evolving roles or creating new roles to grow someone's skill set. We also strategically brought in people with skills the organization had never had. With this approach, we created a team that could bring us to the next level. We challenged ourselves, and each other, to disrupt our leadership style and everything we had ever done.

And, no surprise, it was one of the hardest things we've ever set out to do.

The shift didn't work for everyone. When we upped our game and continued to pursue disruption in all aspects of our business, some people got excited about the opportunities and how the business could grow by using this new approach. Other people were accustomed to working for a small business that had a particular structure. They held on to the old way of doing things; it was hard for them to let go. And yet other people fell somewhere in the middle, and it took us a while to get to know how to work together.

New ideas and systems don't work for everyone. At some point we had to be unafraid to lose people who had been part of the organization for so long, whether it was team members at HeartQuarters (that's what we call our home office) or our franchisees. If the belief wasn't there, we knew it wasn't going to work.

There can be a downside when you really go for what you want, whether personally or professionally, and when you have unapologetic behavior around what you're doing. People either fit or they don't. They either love it or they hate it. And when they really don't fit, they may judge the company or choose to leave. If we want to be bold, we have to be okay with the fact that some people won't like it.

We do believe that if it's not a cultural fit for someone, we need to be in a conversation with them and not shy away from it. So how do we make sure that people always go on to the next stage of their lives and feel great about it?

If someone isn't working out, we never surprise them by pulling the rug out from underneath them. We have conversations about what is working well, what is not working well, what the individual wants and what we need. So we might take longer to let someone go. It's because we want to take that period of time to reflect on the best way to handle the situation. If someone is leaving, what did they learn? What did we learn? Hopefully every part of this process is positive. However, that's not always the case. We endeavor to make it empowering for them to go on and do something else. We also endeavor to empower ourselves to learn how to do better.

An Evolving Culture

In the years I have been with Nurse Next Door, I have had the space to implement Bold Kind people practices that are transforming our business—for our clients and the caregivers and team members who work with us. We are unique because of our transformative people practices and also because, as home care providers, we have firsthand experience of what it means to genuinely care for people (and do so in a way that brings joy to their lives and ensures our business thrives).

I think of this as an ongoing process. It has no ending because we will continue to evolve. Changing culture and people practices doesn't happen overnight. And it shouldn't. When we're shifting our relationships with our team members, it needs to happen naturally and authentically.

In the next chapter, I talk more about how our Bold Kindness efforts are helping us achieve our business goals.

CHAPTER 3

THE BUSINESS OF BOLD KINDNESS

Our franchise development team is in charge of bringing on new franchises to join the Nurse Next Door
brand. We have a strategic, intentionally planned
process that involves signing on new franchises and educating
them about what makes us unique and what we expect from
them. In short, we want to make sure they're a good fit. After
all, if we don't bring on franchisees who are aligned with our
purpose, it doesn't work. Everyone needs to be on board.

For several years in a row, our franchise development team
had been bringing on thirty to fifty new franchises every year,
which was quite respectable. A couple of years ago we sat down
and asked ourselves, *How can we do two hundred deals in a year?*

I get it. That sounds ridiculous, right? That's more than a
four-fold increase in franchise sales. It would be easier to shoot
for a more realistic (and still ambitious) goal of, say, seventy new
franchises a year. At Nurse Next Door, that's not the way we

do things. We don't want to have a preconceived notion of the limits of our goals. We think about how we can push things further and what mindset we need to achieve ambitious, even outrageous, goals. So we stepped into this thought process of: *We could double or triple our lead generation. Why not quadruple it instead?* This is what led to our two-hundred-deal goal.

The truth is that we didn't quite make that goal. (I share our results in a bit.) By coming at the situation from a performance-accelerating mindset versus a performance-limiting mindset, we came much closer than anyone thought possible and blasted through our previous goals. Instead of doing the thing we had always done and sticking with the status quo, we thought about what was wildly possible.

The core value behind this thinking at Nurse Next Door is that we always work to *find a better way.* This is part of our DNA and what we aspire to when we come to work. We promote an entrepreneurial culture where creativity, individual initiative and out-of-the-box thinking is the norm. We search for a better way to provide our services.

How do we find a better way? We sit down as a team and start by clarifying our long-term goal. Then we ask, "What's possible?" We challenge our team to come up with ideas, even if they seem implausible. Or we ask somebody completely outside of the project for their ideas; people who are unfamiliar with a project can often see it more clearly than people who know it intimately.

Another thing we do is walk through every stage of a process, no matter how small it is, and ask ourselves how we can improve it. Is there a glut of emails that are taking up too much of our sales team's time? Let's think about shifting to a messaging platform instead. Are meetings too lengthy? Let's set a strict agenda and make sure everyone shows up on time and is prepared. We catch all the low-hanging fruit, then expand to other areas. Every tiny action we take to improve a process will increase the likelihood we will achieve our goal.

Let's look at the groundwork needed to make it possible to find a better way, then I'll circle back to our two-hundred-deal goal.

Continuous Disruption

The entire basis of Nurse Next Door's business is to be disruptive: to go beyond conventional wisdom and shake up our industry. That means we need to have team members who aren't afraid to challenge the norm.

Let me give you an example. Caregiving has been traditionally viewed as a casual occupation and not something one would think of as a serious career. It generally doesn't pay well, has little job security and provides limited opportunities for career advancement. That's been the traditional model for millions of caregivers working worldwide and a situation that seems, well, impossible to change.

At Nurse Next Door, we don't think this is acceptable. Through an initiative called Caregiving as a Career, we are challenging the norm by working to continuously disrupt our industry and ensure caregivers are respected, valued and well paid. We believe caregiving can, and should, be a long-term career goal. We think caregivers should have job security, benefits and guaranteed hours, and know their employer has their back. We've even gone so far as to revamp our client services agreement to ensure client visits can't be canceled last minute and that caregivers are paid for the time they're booked.

Caregiving as a Career is a really bold initiative! That's the kind of company we are. We don't believe in mediocrity. We aim to disrupt. We step outside our comfort zone and challenge our current reality with a 10x growth mindset. Together we surpass traditional goals by thinking bigger than we currently are and by exponentially leapfrogging our business.

Disruption can be scary. I get it. None of us wants to do something that's going to cost our company lots of money if we fail. So work up to it. Start small.

One of our team members has a friend who is a professor at a major university. It's a very traditional environment, and she felt stifled by the level of uniformity around her. Even the faculty offices on her floor were devoid of any real personality. She wanted to do something to disrupt things and feel a spark of joy. So one evening, after everyone had gone home for the day, she painted her office door bright orange. She was terrified that she would be called out on it and scolded, and she did it anyway. And, sure, some people made comments, but nothing bad happened. Within the year several other professors had painted their doors different colors.

And that led her to doing other disruptive things as well: changing up her curriculum, holding classes on the lawn, coming up with ideas for holding more productive faculty meetings.

And again, some people didn't like it. She was energized and excited, her classes filled up quickly and her Rate My Professors ratings went way up.

All of these actions could have backfired for her. She was confident, she stuck to her guns and the head of her department supported her. This was critical. It's up to all of us as leaders to support our team members in coming up with disruptive actions.

So when our team wants to find a better way of doing something, we ask them, "What's the boldest thing we could do to achieve this goal?" That's our starting point.

Abundance, Not Scarcity

When we are looking at performance acceleration, it's important that we move out of the mindset of scarcity and into a mindset of abundance. Here's what I mean by that. As someone who's a mom and CEO, with lots of things to get done during the day, I might think, *I don't have enough time in the day to do it all.* That's coming from a position of scarcity. When I come from a position of abundance, I reframe it as, *I have two hours in my day to do something I love to do. What do I want to prioritize?*

When I'm in the mindset of abundance, I see *possibilities*. I'm excited and curious. I ask questions. I'm continuously improving, and I'm never satisfied.

Scarcity mindsets, however, start from a negative space. They set us up with preconceived notions about our limitations. When we start in a negative, predetermined space, everything around us reflects that. There is no space to be bold, try new things or forge new ways.

I was once talking to someone about how we at Nurse Next Door believe in paying people more (see chapter 9 for details). This person said their company was struggling and they couldn't afford to pay higher salaries. In saying that, they were coming from a place of fear and scarcity. When we come from a place of scarcity, things seem impossible. Now that might sound like a flippant thing to say, and I genuinely believe it. By coming at things from a place of abundance, we focus on what we have and where we can go. The thought might be, *I have some key people who are incredibly talented. What changes can I make to free up the resources to pay them what they're worth?* When we come from a place of abundance—when we see the possibilities and the talent that's in front of us—we're more likely to find creative solutions.

We can have exponential growth with an Abundance Mindset. We can't have it when we have a mindset that's limited by scarcity.

Now, when COVID hit, it was a hard time for a lot of people. It was scary. And it would have been so easy to bring a negative mindset into our business. I'll admit we had some challenging times, and it was emotionally hard for a lot of people. Before the pandemic hit, we had set a goal of opening two hundred locations in the next year. If we had been in a scarcity mindset during the pandemic, we could have thought, *Hey, this is ridiculous. We're at an unprecedented time in our history when nobody wants to have a stranger inside their home. People are out of work and they're suffering financially. It's not realistic to open up more locations.*

Instead, we stepped into the possibilities. We knew people needed care and that the safest place to be was (and is) at home. What would we need to change to achieve our goal? As I talk about earlier, we did that by bringing our franchise onboarding system online and streamlining processes so we could accelerate growth in an efficient manner. And you know what? A lot of it was due to our team members. They are self-led leaders who have a disruptive mindset, and they carry that infectious energy throughout the organization.

Coming from a place of abundance is also just fun. I remember when I was very young and first started working for a retailer. We had a financial goal for the month end, and as the end of the last day of the month was approaching, we realized we were a bit short. So we got out the phone book, called up our most loyal customers and literally asked them if they wanted to buy something. We told them we'd keep the store open an hour later just for them. These customers came in and bought things, and we ended up surpassing our month-end goal. The best part was that it was so much fun. It felt exhilarating.

Here's another example. We have a call once a month with our financial investors. At one point, we were talking to them about our year-over-year growth. They paused and said, "So hang on. Your year-over-year growth is over 31 percent and you're not happy with that?" And the thing is we're not attached to results. We're neutral. We actually think it could be way more than +31 percent. In the world of business, you *should* be happy with +31 percent. Is that what we want? It's the whole concept of hockey stick growth. We think we can do 150 percent. We're also not attached to the great numbers or the bad numbers. If we're always defining ourselves by the good or the bad, where does that get us?

When I talk about an Abundance Mindset, the fact is that some of our team members won't be on board. It can feel so much safer to come from a scarcity mindset, and it can serve as a well-entrenched self-protective mechanism. And if we have team members who aren't on board, I'm willing to bet they're not self-led leaders. (I talk more about self-led leaders later in this book.)

If we're coming from a place of scarcity, we are not hiring the right people because we're limiting what we pay or the benefits we offer. And we will see lackluster business results as a consequence. Even with self-led leaders, conversations about scarcity can creep in. We watch for those conversations and for our own internal thoughts about abundance and scarcity.

We try to set an example for our team when it comes to this mindset. A lot of it starts by retraining our own brains. When I find myself slipping into a negative mindset, I think, *How can I look at this differently?* As I talk about in the upcoming section on unconventional skills to fuel Bold Kind leadership, I create ways to find balance and calm in my life, so that my mind comes from a place of abundance, not scarcity. And the more I do that, the more others will do the same.

Ongoing Learning

After I finished university, I started working in retail. Most people don't have career aspirations to work in retail. For me, I loved people and I was good at sales. I remember my math teacher from high school actually called me up in the store and said, "What are you doing? You're making a mistake. You have so much more potential."

I actually didn't know what she was talking about. What I saw, that she didn't see, was all of the different things I could do, starting with that role, as long as I worked hard. I mean, I was making $3.75 an hour. What kept me excited was that my own hard work could create opportunities for me. I knew I could control how hard I worked and how disciplined I was, and I was determined to be the best. And that began the long trajectory of a career that ended up with me opening the company's operations in Germany.

And you know what? Even if that first job had been a mistake, it would have been okay. I still would have learned something. If I had been afraid of making a mistake, or afraid of challenging the norm of what I was "supposed" to do, my career would never have happened the way it did.

At Nurse Next Door, we're not afraid to make mistakes. However, what's essential is that when we make a mistake, we learn from it. We don't keep making the same mistake over and over. If people have a good idea, we let them try it out. It's about an aligned-upon goal. We have an aligned-upon goal and then we get out of the way so team members can figure out how to do it. They have parameters for how to get there. It promotes development and thinking, self-led leadership and ownership. It helps them develop confidence.

And if something goes wrong, we don't blame them or pull them from the project. When someone comes to me and says they've made a mistake or they failed, I don't start blaming or judging them. Instead, I ask, "What did you learn?" I come from a place of curiosity. It's only by making mistakes that we learn, understand and continually improve.

The same attitude applies to all of us here at Nurse Next Door, from the senior leaders through to franchisees. The conversation is always about what we have learned. "What can we do differently? What's working and what's not working?" When we take on a mindset of Continuous Improvement, we're able to come up with new ideas and approaches. For example, when we started creating e-learning for our franchises, we didn't just come up with an off-the-shelf solution. Everyone actively contributed feedback on what could make it the best it could be. And we encouraged our team to come up with bold ideas for social media tactics and innovative approaches.

At Nurse Next Door, we welcome our wins and misses. We openly discuss our learnings. We embrace the challenges and mistakes. There's no innovation if we don't do that. I've talked before about mistakes and how tragic it is that many people consider mistakes to be some kind of failure. We have to make it safe for people to take chances. I've always believed we are 100 percent responsible for our communication, results, performance and happiness. No one else will do it for us.

Our Ambitious Franchise Goal

Now back to our ambitious goal of quadrupling our franchise onboarding rate. When challenged with this objective, our franchise development team drew on the themes from this chapter: being disruptive, coming from a mindset of abundance (not scarcity), accepting that mistakes will happen and always looking to find a better way. With these parameters in place, the team got together, examined every piece of the franchise development process and brainstormed solutions. They were willing to adapt and evolve wherever they needed to.

Here's an example. We used to have a live conference call every day at 4pm for prospective franchisees. The team told me the process was archaic. We were pushing prospects to attend the call at a certain time. Nowadays people don't want to wait for a meeting; they want the information immediately.

As a result, the franchise development team created a video that potential franchisees can download and watch whenever they want, 24 hours a day. The team wasn't sure if people would like it, so they didn't get rid of the conference call right away. After three weeks they looked at the data and monitored the results. They found that everyone loved the video and didn't need the conference call, so they eliminated it. Now people can access the video whenever they want to. The team is not spending so much time setting up live meetings. Not only that, they've also substantially grown traffic and leads because people can watch the video 24/7.

The team learned from all the changes they made. They set out steps to accomplish their goal, and they regularly paused to figure out what was and wasn't working. In other words, they were in a state of Continuous Improvement. When they came up with ideas that didn't pan out, their attitude was, "Okay, this didn't work, so let's not do it again. What else can we try?" They approached things with curiosity and from an Abundance Mindset, instead of feeling defeated and giving up.

By the way, as a result of that video initiative, coupled with other improvements to the process, we dramatically accelerated our franchise development program. Now, we didn't reach the two-hundred-deal goal I reference earlier in this chapter. But in our 2020 fiscal year, we sold thirty-three franchises, and in 2021 we sold 114 franchises, more than four times the 2020 figure.

When we empower everyone to contribute and do their best, they come alive and become excited. For the franchise development team, it was by stepping into the space and not being afraid to challenge the norm that we made it happen. To create a massive increase in lead generation, we had to turn it on its head. And when the team fully stepped into it, they looked at things completely differently. They challenged everything.

The fact that we missed the actual goal is less important than the idea that setting an ambitious goal allowed us to achieve results we had never thought possible.

I genuinely believe that the only way to excel in your market, regardless of your business, is by continuously finding a better way. And the only way we can do that is with the support, creativity and ingenuity of our team members.

Do I do better work and achieve more when I do the same thing every day, or when I'm striving to do better? Unless I'm constantly pushing myself to do better, I will remain complacent, and I won't have a competitive edge.

We also have to have the type of culture where we can be vulnerable and shift things when we need to. For instance, at another company I might have created an annual plan and stuck to it, no matter what. Well, at Nurse Next Door we create an annual plan, and if we see an opportunity, we might shift that plan 180 degrees. For some people, that's disconcerting; they would see such a shift as an indication that the company is not organized. For us, it's about being willing to take a chance. It's about being willing to say yes when everyone else is saying no. It's about being willing to give up our position and try something new. This all allows our company to grow faster.

We have to think big to go big.

Inspiring Bold Business Goals

To achieve bold business goals, we have to create an environment where people are not afraid to take risks. Business grows on the calculated risks we take. If we're not taking chances, we're not doing our jobs. Our team shouldn't be afraid to get fired because they try something new. Great things happen when people bring innovative ideas and opportunities to the table.

I'm proud to say that our team members at Nurse Next Door want to continuously improve. We love getting into real conversations about how we can create change. By creating an environment and culture where boldness and kindness come together, we have been able to go above and beyond what we thought was possible.

BOLD KIND REFLECTIONS:
THE BUSINESS OF BOLD KINDNESS

- How can you be more disruptive and challenge the norms in your business?
- If you weren't holding anything back, what would you do?
- How can you bring more of an Abundance Mindset to your life?

PART 2

BOLD KIND SELF

t can be easy to look outside ourselves for answers, or to think that if *other* people changed, our lives would be better. It can be easy to think that if a member of our team just started doing things the way we wanted them to, work would go so much more smoothly. Or if a team member would stop procrastinating about their tasks, everyone would get more done. And while yes, there are often things a team can change to improve performance, we as leaders have to start with how *we* show up and lead others, what we enable our team to do/not do and what mindset we are leading with.

In fact, one of the most important lessons I've learned is that if I focus too much on changing the people around me, I ignore the true driver of change: *me*. Over the years, I have learned that change has to start from within. I realized I could not expect others to take action when I wasn't doing the same for myself. To be a Bold Kind leader, I needed to focus on developing my Bold Kind self.

What is a Bold Kind self? Being calm and caring. Being curious about myself and where I can grow. Cultivating purpose and being true to myself. And, as a leader, having the courage to disrupt our business and create ambitious goals.

In my own life, I know I control what I do. If I'm not focusing first on myself or coming from a place of integrity, I'm not being real with myself. If I am not happy or satisfied with my life, it's going to be reflected in how I show up with my team. They are directly affected by how I speak, what I think and how I show up. My behavior as a leader and individual shapes how others behave. For example, if my team is showing up late to meetings, or if they're unprepared and not contributing, I have to start by asking myself some questions. *Why are they showing up this way? How am I showing up, and how is my behavior aligning with what I say? Do I need to set different expectations or give feedback to the team?* I have to know myself, understand my strengths and opportunities and feel confident in being *me* before I can lead a team of people who depend on me. I think the same is true for all of us.

That's why Bold Kindness has to start with the self. We have to look honestly at our strengths and challenges and where we need to grow. As I went through this work, I identified eight key principles to Bold Kind self: things that have most helped me effect change in myself and ultimately my team. They fall into three categories:

1. Showing up as a fully expressed self

    ◦ Principle 1: Belonging to ourselves

    ◦ Principle 2: Being vulnerable

    ◦ Principle 3: Being curious

2. Unconventional skills to fuel Bold Kind leadership

- ◦ Principle 4: Intuitive listening
- ◦ Principle 5: White space and balance
- ◦ Principle 6: Thinking lean

3. Leadership commitments of a Bold Kind leader
   - ◦ Principle 7: Connecting to purpose
   - ◦ Principle 8: Disrupting with intention

These are principles that I've developed from working with my leadership team, who have been an amazing part of creating the Nurse Next Door brand. We learn from each other every day. In the following chapters, I explore each of these principles and demonstrate how they provide a solid foundation for becoming a Bolder Kinder self.

CHAPTER 4

SHOWING UP AS A
FULLY EXPRESSED SELF

When I come to work, I show up as Cathy. Mother, daughter, CEO, tennis player, runner. I'm not just Cathy the CEO. I can laugh, joke around, be serious or be quiet, depending on how I feel, not how I think I should be. I start meetings by asking others how they are, if they had a good weekend or if they are having fun working on a project. It is a kinder, more caring way of working with my team.

What I love about Bold Kindness is that it centers on transparency and openness. These are traits we must embrace as individuals before we can expect the rest of our organizations to follow suit.

For me, transparency and openness are symbolized by a couch in my office. . . .

Creating a Caring Environment

When I first came on board at Nurse Next Door, there was a couch in my office. And I kept it because I liked the idea of creating a space that felt less businesslike and more inviting. Over time, I simply stopped sitting at the desk in my office. The couch became a natural place to gravitate to, and it is an amazing place to have meaningful conversations.

A couch creates a feeling of home and a caring environment. This concept fits in beautifully with our work at Nurse Next Door. We're in the business of caring for people, and that commitment to care extends beyond our clients to caregivers, franchisees and the HeartQuarters (head office) team. I'd argue that *all* businesses are in the business of caring for people. Caring for my team and clients is a key component of what I do.

When I have a conversation with a team member, we sit next to each other on the couch. We break apart the traditional model in which I sit in a big, comfortable chair at a big, impressive desk, while the team member sits across from me in a smaller, less comfortable chair, separated from me by my huge desk. And because of the less formal environment, we end up having a real conversation—just two people sitting on the couch chatting. Some of our best ideas come from working on the couch. We empower people to think outside of the box—and make themselves a little mentally uncomfortable—by inviting them to get physically comfortable.

THE COUCH EFFECT

By way of a preview of what I talk about in part 3, it comes as no surprise to me that more comfortable workplaces mean happier and more engaged team members.[4] It takes more than just financial incentives to keep people satisfied. Whether it's getting rid of cubicles, letting in more natural light or offering different spaces for the team to work in, office design is underrated. Seemingly insignificant things like furniture or windows that open can affect our physical, functional and psychological comfort. For some people, these features might be photos, plants or a pool table. For me, it's a couch. By having conversations on my couch, I'm most genuine and vulnerable, without having a barrier between myself and others. It encourages an equal playing field and makes it easier to openly share ideas and collaborate.

What I also realized over time is that the physical structure of the couch helps create open and real conversations; it removes barriers that are both physical and emotional. As a result, it encourages team members—myself included—to embrace who we are and have heart-to-heart conversations. In my experience,

---

4   N. Kamarulzaman, A.A. Saleh, S.Z. Hashim, H. Hashim, A.A. Abdul-Ghani, "An Overview of the Influence of Physical Office Environments Towards Employee," Procedia Engineering (2011): 262–268, https://www.sciencedirect.com/science/article/pii/S1877705811029730.

it has allowed those sitting in my office to feel more comfortable—like being at home—so it opens us up to being vulnerable. And I believe that being vulnerable is such an essential part of being a good leader. It helps break down the hierarchical walls of leadership to allow for connection and relationships.

Okay, I know I'm talking about the couch a lot. Here's the thing: Sitting on a couch and having a chat brings back the simplicity of being a real person. It welcomes connection and trust and demonstrates vulnerability. That's who I am. The first three principles in my list of eight are key to showing up with my full humanity on display:

- Belonging to ourselves
- Being vulnerable
- Being curious

Principle 1: Belonging to Ourselves

It's interesting to me that in the business world, when we're describing ourselves on a resume or a bio, we often talk about accomplishments: things like education and degrees, job experience, awards, that type of thing. Which makes sense. What's missing is something deeper than that: identifying specific personal and business skills in which you excel.

I believe doing so is important because it's those inherent qualities and skills that make us unique business leaders.

Part of being a great leader means knowing what we're good at and what we're not good at, then building a team around us that complements that. I also think that by recognizing the strengths within us, we're able to cultivate more confidence and sense of who we are as individuals, which motivates and inspires those around us. Most of all, we remain true to ourselves, instead of trying to make ourselves adapt to some external vision of who we think we should be.

Here's the thing: When I am aligned with my values and who I am, my team knows me and trusts me. If I want people to be fair and respectful with one another, and to challenge their ways of thinking, I have to do the same. If I want them to be resilient and to push themselves harder when things get challenging, I have to be willing to roll up my sleeves and do it as well.

I learned the importance of being bold and standing up for myself and what I believe in. And listen, it wasn't easy. It still isn't. I still struggle. I still don't have all of the answers, and I am excited to be on this learning journey. Other people in Nurse Next Door have felt the same, as you'll see in Kelly's story.

Kelly's story

Kelly, our Director, People & Culture, has been with Nurse Next Door for more than ten years and first joined our team when she was twenty-three years old. Over the past decade, Kelly has actively developed her skill set and taken on a number of roles to challenge herself and continue to grow. She is a true learner and always curious about following her passions and instincts.

We fully support this because this is what we do here: We actively develop people, help challenge their thinking and expand their skill sets.

A few years after Kelly started, some new team members were brought into the organization. Kelly initially assumed that because they had extensive HR experience, they knew more than she did. She began doubting herself and her abilities and questioned her role at Nurse Next Door. She had a gut feeling about how things should be done, and she didn't have the confidence to bring her voice to the table.

Since we are a people development culture, we care for our people. So we sat down with her and talked openly about it. The team saw this as a great time to continue developing Kelly and help her pursue her interest and passion in HR. So we arranged for Kelly to continue to grow and expand her skill set by gaining more experience in the HR realm. We did it in a very unconventional way. We had a great relationship with a local company and enabled her to work there for a while to gain experience. We continued to pay her salary while she was away. She worked for a few months in their HR and Culture department and learned about their work processes, culture and people practices. We held Kelly's role until she returned.

When she came back to Nurse Next Door, Kelly had developed an even greater breadth of skills and experience. She had acquired even more than that. She had learned to recognize her own strengths. She felt confident in following her gut instincts and calling something out when it didn't feel right. She knew that even though she might not have as many years of experience as other team members, she had an invaluable understanding and connection with our culture. She continues to be an essential member of our team and now helps mentor others on following their passion and recognizing their own strengths.

Wanting to embrace Bold Kindness means knowing yourself and being self-aware, with an openness to posing tough questions (to yourself and others). Self-reflection can be challenging at times. I have learned that I have to be intuitive and open to challenging myself, to wanting to learn and grow.

I have found there are two questions I need to ask myself over and over again so I can really dig deep into who I am and how I'm showing up.

How do I accept and value myself?

The first thing I ask myself is: *How do I accept and value myself?*

I could easily spend a lot of time thinking about how to improve myself and to figure out how to overcome challenges. I can (and still do!) spend a lot of time trying to "fix what's wrong." It can be really easy for me to go to the negative parts of my personality and life and to figure out how to fix what I don't want. I actually think we spend too much time trying to fix what's wrong. Let's stop trying to fix ourselves.

The truth is that every quality has a positive and negative aspect. Someone who is great at organizing might be a bit controlling. Someone who's empathetic might also be a pushover. We're all a combination of strengths and opportunities: things we love, others we don't.

And that's okay. It's not about getting it right; it's about being more of who you already are.

I really try to spend more time embracing my own strengths and what makes me truly energized and unique. I think about two of the principles of Happier Aging at Nurse Next Door: Belonging and Respect. Belonging is about accepting myself for who I am. When I do, I feel a greater sense of fulfillment, well-being and belonging. It connects me with something bigger than myself. And when I respect myself and others, I demonstrate care, concern and consideration.

This first question—*How do I accept and value myself?*—is important for cultivating a sense of belonging and purpose. It helps us recognize and take pride in our strengths and to accept, even embrace, our weaknesses.

Where do I want to grow?

This may sound paradoxical since I just said that we should start by trying not to fix ourselves. That doesn't mean we should accept the status quo. There is always room for improvement. So the second question I ask myself is: *Where do I want to grow as a leader and human being?*

The answer will be unique to each of us, and it could involve personal traits or business traits. When we recognize where we want to grow, we are able to cultivate the skills we need, whether that's internally (cultivating them within) or externally (hiring people who have the skills that we don't). For instance, I'm working on being more peaceful and patient, as those aren't my strongest skills. I recognize that those are areas where I want to continue to grow.

I'm also a huge proponent of hiring people who are better than me, which is one form of external improvement. The people who surround me are *far* better at their tasks than I am, and I rely on them to help achieve our business goals. I hire my weakness. Then I try to get out of the way and let *them* tell *me* what to do.

Acknowledging our weaknesses or gaps can be one of the hardest things we can do. Answering this question requires a lot of honesty, and we may or may not like the answers we get. It takes courage and humility to understand where we need support, and it may be downright scary.

BOLD KIND REFLECTIONS: BELONGING TO OURSELVES

- What would living an exceptional life look like?
- What is your daily source of energy and joy?
- What are you best in the world at? What is your superpower?

Principle 2: Being Vulnerable

Somebody once told me that I continuously put myself in challenging situations. And that is a really big piece of what I have done in my life to develop myself. If I'm not uncomfortable, I'm uncomfortable. In my retail days, the company I worked for asked me if I'd rather stay where I was (Edmonton, Alberta) and wait for the next door to open up, or move to Saskatoon, Saskatchewan (a third the size of Edmonton) because there was an opportunity there. Everyone thought I was crazy when I drove to Saskatoon with my two cats in my back seat. I opened myself up to possibility. Enjoying challenges is part of the fullest version of myself. That's why I challenge myself to do more introspection and make myself open and vulnerable.

What does it mean to be vulnerable? To me, it means showing up as the real Cathy; it means allowing myself to feel, acknowledge and show my emotions without guilt or worry of judgment. Being vulnerable means being real and authentic.

I believe that vulnerability is key to being a Bold Kind leader and humanizing the workplace. When you show your vulnerability, other people feel encouraged to be real about their own feelings. When we as leaders are open about who we are and share personal stories—what happened, what we learned, what we still need to learn—it breaks down the barriers. And when someone understands that other people might be struggling, and they're not the only one, it gives them strength.

It gives them energy and desire to embrace who they are, let barriers down and remove fear from what they are doing so that they can thrive. And yes, I think it can be hard for people to open themselves up if they haven't done it before. It's realizing it's okay to be willing to expose your feelings or express what you really think, no matter how unwelcome or unpopular it might be. It's about stepping into fear and doing it anyway.

Vulnerability is particularly important when times are tough. When things are hard, we need to show up in a state of openness, with a willingness to acknowledge our emotions. We need to be real. You know, when you think about it, we are all going through life together. I think that's a really important part of this. And we're only going to be more connected with one another if we're honest about what we're going through and share our stories. Here's how one of our team members found her own path to vulnerability.

Yvette's story

Too often people believe, think or are taught that they can only show their professional side at work.

One of our team members, Yvette, had lived in Eastern Canada for more than forty years. She came west to Vancouver following the loss of her seventeen-year-old daughter. When she joined Nurse Next Door, she was determined to not tell anyone about her recent loss; she didn't want anyone to treat her differently. She was also firmly convinced she should keep one version of herself at home and have a separate version of herself for work. She believed the two should never blend or overlap.

We wanted to make her feel comfortable and let her know she didn't have to hide herself away. Nurse Next Door has a work culture where vulnerability is encouraged: We openly talk about our feelings and encourage our team members to be open. When we ask, "How are you today?" and someone responds with "Okay," we don't move on. We ask them what is going on, and if they'd like to share it.

For Yvette, coming to Nurse Next Door was a bit of a culture shock. She initially struggled with our culture because it was so foreign to her, and she had become used to suppressing the feelings of grief she had been carrying.

At one point Yvette and her leader were having a very open conversation and Yvette felt very upset. Then she had a breakthrough moment: She was either going to leave the organization or allow herself to stay and be vulnerable. Yvette chose to share how she felt. She shared her story with team members. She talked about how incredibly scary it is to be vulnerable at work with people she sees every day. And it changed everything for her. She felt free to speak her mind and to tell everyone she needed a moment if she was having a bad day.

"Being vulnerable and open took so much weight off my shoulders," she told me. "I don't have to pretend to be someone I'm not or to hide my feelings. I can have more empathy for myself and my team members. I know that if I don't bring my whole self to work, I can't give my whole self to whatever I am doing."

I understand where Yvette was coming from. My husband was sick for quite a while before he died, which was an extremely difficult time in my life. I deliberately didn't shut it away. I showed up at work, sat on the couch with my team and some days I cried. I didn't think too much about why I was doing it at the time. It helped me show up as a wife, mother and CEO all at once and to express vulnerability and pain for what I was going through. I didn't want to stay at home and tuck that version of myself away in private.

BOLD KIND REFLECTIONS: BEING VULNERABLE

- What does being vulnerable feel like to you?
- What's the greatest lesson you've learned in your own life?
- Think of a time you worked at something you were not good at. How did it feel? What did you learn?

Principle 3: Being Curious

I believe that curiosity is about being a continuous learner: asking questions, learning new skills and increasing knowledge. After all, no matter how much experience I may have, I always have something to learn.

I have learned that when I am genuinely curious about who I am and where I'm going, so much opens up. If I'm not sure about something we are doing, I ask *why*. And then, when I have the answer to that, I ask *why* some more. By being curious and not staying stuck in my ways, I open myself up to possibility.

Curiosity is the opposite of judgment. For example, when I first joined Nurse Next Door as President in 2014, I thought it was interesting that very few people did the dishes. I would arrive at the office in the morning and there would be dishes in the sink . . . unrinsed plates, coffee cups, a dirty storage container. You get the picture. This isn't a slight against Nurse Next Door or how things were before I arrived; it just was what it was. It's a pretty typical scenario at most companies. Large offices tend to have more people, and the communal responsibilities of office cleanup get lost in the busy hustle and bustle of the day-to-day.

A natural reaction to this situation would have been to get a bit irritated. I could have said to the team, "Excuse me, do your dishes!" Instead of getting cross about it, I rolled up my sleeves and did the dishes. For weeks, I did the dishes every day. And people noticed. Simultaneously, I got curious. I focused on trying to understand *why* no one was doing the dishes. *Why did people think it wasn't their responsibility? Why did they think it wasn't important?* Eventually, I came to realize that this inattention to dirty dishes was a small symptom of a larger issue related to personal responsibility. I didn't find a solution by standing in judgment of people. I found it by being curious and finding the root cause (more on this story in chapter 7).

Far too often we judge actions critically: both our own actions and those of others. A Bold Kind leader needs to fight against that tendency and instead try to look at things objectively, pragmatically and scientifically. What makes something work? Why is it doing what it's doing? What would happen if I experimented with doing things another way?

Curiosity is also essential for disruption. It is impossible to come up with new ideas and push myself to grow unless I'm constantly asking myself questions about what's going on. I think of it like a business problem. What are we trying to solve? What's the boldest way we could do this better? What happened this morning that I can learn from? When I come at things from a place of curiosity, the world opens up.

BOLD KIND REFLECTIONS:
BEING CURIOUS

- What are you curious about?
- Who we are is how we lead. Who are you?
- How do you build a profile of curiosity?

The Fullest Version of Ourselves

I believe that to be a Bold Kind leader, the most important thing I can do is show up as my fully expressed self every day—the personal and professional parts, the organized parts and the vulnerable parts, the quirky and the serious. I'm a mom and a mentor and a friend. I'm a golfer and a runner. When I show up as the fullest version of myself, I make better, more authentic decisions—decisions that aren't guided by ego or fears or hierarchies.

So I challenge you to bring your full self to work and encourage your team members to do the same. Embrace who you are as a person, have the courage to appear vulnerable and emphasize curiosity over judgment. This is the best way to create a solid foundation for having a Bold Kind organization.

CHAPTER 5

UNCONVENTIONAL SKILLS TO FUEL BOLD KIND LEADERSHIP

One of the things I learned on my journey to becoming a Bold Kind leader was that I needed to strengthen skills and focus on talents that aren't always emphasized in a traditional work environment. These are captured by the next set of principles:

- Principle 4: Intuitive listening
- Principle 5: White space and balance
- Principle 6: Thinking lean

Principle 4: Intuitive Listening

I was at a global retail organization for a number of years before moving to Nurse Next Door. They are very different industries:

One is retailing and the other is home care franchising. Retail is a very structured, centralized environment and is operated under one roof. Home care franchising is the opposite: You have hundreds of different home care business owners who own and operate their own franchise, under a common brand.

I remember thinking about the difference between the two industries, and whether I was capable of making the change. And at first I felt like an impostor at Nurse Next Door. I was moving away from something I had been doing for years and going into an entirely different kind of business.

I could have sat back and thought, *Oh, I don't have franchising experience, so I can't do this.* I knew that if I did that, and accepted the story I was telling myself, I wouldn't feel like I was learning, growing and trying something new.

At that moment, I knew I needed to have a conversation with myself. And I realized that on one hand, focusing on the differences in the industries made it uncomfortable for me. On the other hand, when I started thinking of my situation in a different way, I saw that by moving to Nurse Next Door, I'd be continuing to do what I love: working with people. I love making a difference in people's lives. I love working with a purpose. I love being able to work with an awesome team and help people be successful. I realized that I shouldn't focus so much on the differences when moving from retail to franchising; the change was about taking my work with people to a different level.

It's about listening to ourselves more in order to make the right choices. Nobody can make choices for me or determine what I should do. And when I think about finding the commonalities that underlie what I love, no matter what that is—I make the right choice. For me, it's not about having an MBA or a particular type of experience. It's about knowing myself and continuously learning every day. It's about stepping into new and challenging situations. It's about making a choice that feels uncomfortable and doing it anyway. That's when I thrive. It's not about sitting in that classroom and getting that credential. It's about putting myself out there and taking chances.

I love how one of Nurse Next Door's Happier Aging principles is "Choice: doing what you want to do when you want to do it." Having the freedom to choose allows you to shape your life. I feel most empowered when I have a choice. As leaders, we have to demonstrate by our beliefs and actions that everyone is faced with choices and we must each own our confidence, listen to our intuition and stop second-guessing ourselves.

That means listening to our gut. In my own experience, when I listen to my gut, I actually know what I should do. In traditional business environments, I was not taught to trust my intuition, to step into that. Many decisions that leaders face do not fall neatly within defined policies and procedures; the world (and business) is not black and white. We need to spend more time really seeing and hearing and using our intuition. It's important to get rid of the noise and connect with ourselves.

MOVING ON FROM MISTAKES

As I talk about in chapter 3, being disruptive and getting curious is part of Bold Kindness. And when we are disruptive and make bold changes, sometimes mistakes are made. That's okay. In fact, it's more than okay. Mistakes are part of learning. And equally important is learning how to move on from those mistakes. None of us is perfect; mistakes are part of the process of living. They're to be expected. Too often we view mistakes as failures and let them get the better of us.

I make mistakes every day. I'm making choices and I'm making decisions, and some of them are going to be right and some of them are going to be wrong. At the end of the day, I'm just making a choice. That's half the battle, isn't it? If I took them personally and beat myself up, I'd come from a place of negative, self-defeating behavior. Instead, I ask myself: *What can I learn from this experience? How can I help myself grow?* I learn from that and then I move on.

When faced with a choice that seems like the most vulnerable thing I can imagine, that's when it's awesome. I don't want to worry about what anyone else thinks, or what the world wants me to do (which can be the easier thing to do). This is a skill that requires work. Listen to your intuition and go for it. When you listen to your gut, you're connecting with your purpose.

When I was younger, I sometimes didn't go in the direction that my intuition was telling me to go. I might have made a different choice because I didn't think I had the experience or because I listened to someone else. Afterward, I invariably wondered why I didn't trust my instinct.

I would say I've gotten better at that. I need to let myself step into it and shape my thoughts: *I understand this situation because I worked hard and I did these things and I believe in my gut. I believe in my decision-making and I'm going to step in and make that choice.* It's very powerful when I allow myself to do that. That's what helps me be a better mentor and a better person that people can look up to. I have to work on that every day.

Even if I'm unsure, my approach is to take a chance anyway. If there are two options and I am not sure which one to pursue, I ask myself: *Which one is the hardest and makes me most uncomfortable?* I take the hard, uncomfortable route.

If I feel like I don't know what to do or can't feel what's right in my gut, I know I need to spend more time with myself: increasing my awareness, being quiet and looking internally. I talk more about this later. I find it imperative to create white space in my life to discover what is important. I need to go on a walk and reflect. That's how I get moments of clarity—through silence. And in that silence I might find the tiniest nugget of something: a desire, a feeling. So I go there. And from that place, I might see something else. I focus on my curiosity and see where it takes me. I get more information to follow my passion. I have faith in the process. I don't try to make something up or make it bigger or smaller than it needs to be.

The thing is, choices are up to each of us as individuals. No one else should have to give us anything in order to make that happen. It's very liberating when you stop requiring permission or approval from other people and fully step into that. You can get to a place where you think, *I own my confidence. I own whether or not I think I'm doing a good job. I don't need to look externally.* All of a sudden it changes your viewpoint on how you feel about yourself.

BOLD KIND REFLECTIONS: INTUITIVE LISTENING

- How do you tap into your intuition?
- What do you need to embrace?
- What is your biggest source of inspiration?

Principle 5: White Space and Balance

When I ask people how they're doing, I commonly hear the response: "I'm good. Just busy!" It seems that saying we're busy is a normal automatic response. Saying this has become a badge of honor: a statement to the world that says our jobs and our lives are so important that we don't have time to slow down. Technology, social media and smartphones have only made us busier and take over our lives from the moment we get up until the moment we go to sleep.

In today's business environment, leaders often treat business as a list of tasks: things that need to be checked off, such as responding to emails, attending weekly meetings or submitting reports. Quantity is prioritized over quality. Lists and tasks can create a feeling of being rushed; people focus on checking off their to-do items and adding more to the list. There is a sense of urgency to finish it all by the end of the business day, only to start that list again the next day. We miss the moment. We miss what is going on with the people around us.

When I first started at Nurse Next Door, I was stepping into the role of President, taking over for our two cofounders, and I knew I had a lot to learn. However, instead of feeling over-whelmed, I got curious. I took the time I needed to learn and understand the way things worked. I got to know the cofounders and why they set things up the way they did. I didn't speed up; I slowed down. I learned the systems and processes. I met with our franchisees across North America and learned about their journeys, wins and opportunities. I connected with team members at HeartQuarters and learned about their roles and challenges. I really wanted to understand the secret sauce of the company, as well as areas of opportunity for propelling the company forward. And that took time.

I also knew that I couldn't solve every opportunity in one go. I tried to be very thoughtful in the approaches I took and ensure the right conversations were had. I knew I had to create space for me to think this through.

I firmly believe we need to get away from this mentality of being busy. It just doesn't work anymore. It only makes us more stressed and frenetic. We're on the go all the time, and we rarely stop to think about what we're doing. We rarely stop to reflect and simply *be*. This feeling of being rushed can easily stop us from being multidimensional, especially when it comes to other areas in our lives that really make us happy.

The concept of white space

White space is a fundamental concept in art and design. It's the area around objects in photos. It's the unpainted parts of a canvas. It's the spaces between letters. It's blank margins and empty spaces. Without enough white space, design is too overwhelming and hard to digest.

White space is also fundamental to our lives. It's the times when we're meditating, observing our breath or contemplating nature. It's sitting and doing absolutely nothing. And we don't do enough of it. Even when we're "relaxing," we're on our phones, reading or chatting with friends. When we take time for ourselves and create white space in our day-to-day lives, we give ourselves breathing room.

White space is important because it allows our minds to meander. Look at nature; nature meanders. The way it starts isn't the way it ends. A river will always meander and find the simplest route with ease and flow. That's a very different concept than business. Using the simplest route with ease and flow is not the traditional business approach. When we blend the concept of nature with business, magical things can happen.

And it's in that space, where I'm seemingly doing nothing, that everything can happen. When I create space, I can actually be awake for my life. I get perspective. I see things more clearly. My brain is free to solve problems that have been plaguing me, and I'm able to come up with ideas. I create a yin to my yang, a calm to my energy.

Over time, I had to learn to show up differently. Part of being an effective leader is creating white space. I don't think that every hour of the day should be packed with meetings and work activities. Part of the week should be about self-growth: taking time for ourselves. So I make sure to ask myself: *Am I adding white space into my week? Or am I just going about the tactics of my job?*

I also think I need white space when things aren't going well. When I'm having a bad day, I try to create white space. I'll go running or take a walk. I try not to talk too much or make major decisions. I try to be more neutral.

Creating balance

The companion to white space is balance: finding balance in my life. Everyone has their own definition of balance. For me, that is spending time with my family and making sure that I'm spending time in nature. I would say that I make some of the best decisions for the organization, for myself as a person and for my family when I'm out there running and just letting my brain wander. I create the space to meander and come up with bold ideas I hadn't thought of before.

And listen, I love getting excited about life and about where I want the business to go. It's great to have goals and to wake up every morning wanting to make them happen. Thing is, some-times I can get so performance-oriented that it gets too frenetic. This is when I take a step back and slow down.

During the pandemic at Nurse Next Door, we all slowed down. And that was a good thing. I think going slow allows a little more time to stop and reflect, to be present and find more things that bring us meaning, purpose and joy.

I get it. It's really hard to slow down. We've got businesses to run and families to take care of. It can take a while to retrain our brains into understanding that not only is it *okay* to slow down, it also helps us be *stronger*. If it feels too daunting, it can be help-ful just to take small, purposeful steps to start you along the way.

Strategies for balance

Here are some strategies I recommend for slowing down and opening up time for more thinking and for more meaningful conversations.

- **Stop overbooking.** When things get too busy and I realize I need to slow down, I thin out my calendar and stop planning my entire day. I leave time to reflect. I now never schedule meetings or appointments during lunch. Lunch is a time for me to take a moment to reflect on my morning: wins, challenges and conversations I've had. This leaves an opportunity to do more in the afternoon. To implement this idea for yourself, look at your calen-dar. Do you really want or need to be in every meeting listed there?

- **Empower others to do more by leading less.** Several years back we introduced the concept of self-led leadership at Nurse Next Door. I elaborate more on that in the coming chapters. Implementing this concept has allowed me to slow down and do more. I lead *less* to lead *more*. Intstead of focusing my time and energy on the day-to-day things, I focus on developing leaders within our teams who will have a much larger impact on the organization. I only involve myself with the day-to-day when I am asked. Think about the issues or projects you're tackling and ask if you are micromanaging them. Can you allow your team to have more autonomy? (I cover this topic more in the last chapter on mentoring.)

- **Have an open door.** There are a few different things I do to eliminate barriers and create space with team members. I have an open-door policy: People can come in whenever they need to talk to me, and we sit on the couch and chat. They don't need to have an appointment or schedule time with me. And because I no longer plan my day in such an intense way, I can focus on connecting with the team. I do a daily office walk on the floor just to chat with everyone. This not only helps me form connections with team members, it also gives me an opportunity to see what they're up to in the moment, instead of only getting project updates at meetings, where I might miss some of the nuances. Does the idea of having an open-door policy make you apprehensive or excited? If you're worried about interruptions, try scheduling some open-door time every afternoon. If that works out—and as you eliminate more non-value-added meetings from your calendar—you can expand the hours.

- **Take time to do things you love.** For me that is being active, traveling and spending time with family and friends. We don't have to travel far; we just travel when we can. I cherish quality time with them as I am able to be fully present. I put on hold any other roles I assume. We try to see new places and try new things. This broadens my worldview and allows me to approach different situations with perspective and empathy, which ultimately makes me a more efficient and multidimensional leader. And, when I spend time with my family, my attention is fully placed on them. This provides a reference to help me bring the same level of patience, empathy, care and energy to others, such as my team in the office. By being multidimensional and engaging in things that make me happy, I can slow down by appreciating things from a different perspective and a different place of passion/ purpose. What activities make you happy that you'd like to make time for in your busy life? What would it take to make it happen?

BOLD KIND REFLECTIONS: WHITE SPACE AND BALANCE

- What does balance feel like for you?
- What do you love to do? What is important to you?
- Time is finite. Where do you give your time and energy?

Principle 6: Thinking Lean

When I wake up on a Saturday morning and it's cold and pouring rain, the last thing I want to do is put on my running shoes and go outside. Going running on a rainy Saturday morning is really not the first place I would choose to be. Pretty much all of the time, without exception, I do it. It's important to me: I know it's going to help me clear my head and will keep me strong and healthy. And it's only by doing it on a regular basis that I'm going to *stay* strong and clear and healthy. So I do it even when it's tough. I do it *especially* when it's tough. I go running because I know it's going to help me come in to work on Monday and really show up as a strong leader. I stay disciplined with this because I believe it is essential to my well-being.

The concept of self-discipline has been drummed into our heads for a long time. "Do your homework so you get good grades" or "Pay your bills on time so you don't get bad credit." Self-discipline is essential because *it's how we get things done*. For me, when I think of self-discipline, I go somewhere else. When I think of self-discipline, I always go to the word *lean*.

A lean business leader maximizes value while minimizing waste. They focus on improving processes and efficiencies. Lean leadership isn't about things like cutting costs or firing people. It's about eliminating unnecessary behaviors, mindsets, processes and practices, so we're not bogged down in things that are unimportant.

Strategies for thinking lean

I believe thinking lean is an essential part of being a Bold Kind leader because it helps drive efficiency, performance and focus. Here are some of the strategies I use to stay lean:

- **Keep a lean environment.** This is the business equivalent of keeping my house clean. I find that by keeping my environment lean and simple, I have less room for distraction. I have more physical space around me to think clearly. When I keep my workspace clean, my headspace is also clean and clear. It sends a message to myself that *my space matters.*

- **Do what needs to be done.** It takes way more energy to procrastinate or put off a task than to just do it. I try not to overthink about whether or not something is worthwhile. If it is, I do it. If it's not, I let it go. The way I see it is that I'll either have a small disappointment now (if I make myself do the thing) or a bigger disappointment later (if I don't do what I promised myself I would).

- **Mindfully show up.** I think we need to be mindful about how we show up for ourselves before we can be aware of how we show up for others. By showing up for myself in a mindful way, I learn a lot about self-discipline. I'm not wasting time or energy on unnecessary interactions. For instance, I think about how I show up as a mother. As a mother, I have to think about my behavior and how I'm impacting my children. I want to be the best version of myself with my kids and to be very conscious when I haven't shown up in the way I want to. I feel the same way about how I show up with the people on my team.

- **Be connected.** To think lean, I need to be myself. It takes too much energy to pretend to be someone I'm not, especially when I'm with other people. I might ask myself: *Have I built a relationship with this person so I can be honest in this conversation? If not, how can I change that so I can feel free to be my truest self?*

BOLD KIND REFLECTIONS: THINKING LEAN

- What do you say yes to in your life that causes chaos?
- Where is there waste or inefficiency in your life?
- What is the one habit you want to break, and what is the one habit you want to create?

Leadership Skills Not Taught in Business School

Business school teaches us all kinds of valuable skills essential for running a business. However, business courses typically don't teach us about listening to our gut, creating white space and balance, having a lean mentality or being focused and disciplined. I feel strongly that these are essential skills for people who want to approach leadership with Bold Kindness. Bold Kind skills help us maintain perspective through good times and bad. They help us project the right mentality when dealing with the people whose lives we want to shape. They make us more adaptable and flexible as leaders. They help our businesses and teams shine.

CHAPTER 6

LEADERSHIP COMMITMENTS OF A BOLD KIND LEADER

I n part 3, I describe a number of specific strategies that leaders can employ to create an environment where everyone can be the fullest version of themselves and convert that positive energy into business results.

All of that work starts with how we lead. That's why, in this chapter, I want to talk about the commitments that are essential for each of us as leaders, so we are prepared to actually lead our organizations in a new direction. They are reflected in the last two principles:

- Principle 7: Connecting to purpose
- Principle 8: Disrupting with intention

Principle 7: Connecting to Purpose

Do you believe in your company's purpose and culture? Does it align with your vision and purpose for your own life? If not,

it will be difficult to be a Bold Kind leader. How can you promote and drive a culture of Bold Kindness without believing
in the purpose of the company?

I talk more about this in chapter 7. In the meantime, take
time to fully understand your purpose as an individual and figure out how it aligns with that of your organization. This sounds
like a simple task, doesn't it? On our team, we have to create
space for ourselves to live and breathe the culture. And I think
this is key, particularly when I'm a new leader at an organization.
How do I make sure I respect and embody the company's mission and purpose? Do I believe in it?

For example, as I note earlier, before I came to Nurse Next
Door, I spent a lot of time working for a publicly traded retail
business. Nurse Next Door, though, is completely different. It is a
privately held company led by founders who have created a secret
sauce and are directly involved in its success. I had to pay attention to that. I needed to think about how I could contribute to
Nurse Next Door in a meaningful way and not lose sight of their
vision. So in my first few months with Nurse Next Door, I spent
a significant amount of time learning their vision for the future. I
took time to understand and experience it. I had to "go slow to go
fast" to make sure I respected and nourished the culture.

I had to leverage what had been created, and not lose sight
of it. When I look at why so many executives are not successful
going into these roles, I feel like it's because they think they are
better than the brand that has been created. I had to spend a lot of
my time making sure that I understood the culture, the brand and
the vision. I needed to stay humble and be a continuous learner.

It's very similar to moving to another country. As mentioned earlier in the book, when I was first starting my career, I found myself living in Germany for three years, running the operations of a global retail organization. And in going to a new country and a new culture, I had to remind myself to be humble. I had to learn and understand a completely different way of life and to revere and respect that culture. If I had fought against it and tried to do everything the way they do it in Canada, it wouldn't have worked. And it's the same way with any business.

BOLD KIND REFLECTIONS: CONNECTING TO PURPOSE

- What difference do you want to make? What impact do you want to have?
- How meaningful is your work?
- How do you want people to feel when they walk through the door?

Principle 8: Disrupting with Intention

The concept of business disruption has been around for a while: using nonconventional business models and tactics to accelerate business growth. In an era shaped by the Internet, social media and start-ups, it's a time when anything goes. Business models are being turned on their head.

Which is great. I love that. I truly believe that to stand out as leaders, we have to be brave, vulnerable and disruptive. When I go with the status quo, I get mediocrity. When I go with safe, I get safe. And when I do that, I don't grow. I don't take chances. I believe that I need to say yes when everyone else is saying no. Disruption means asking myself what I need to say yes to that is challenging, uncomfortable and out of the box.

Nowhere did those adjectives come together more clearly than in the commitment we made to build a culture of Bold Kindness at Nurse Next Door. The idea of Bold Kindness was radically new for everyone. And I pursued it because I really believe in the concept of self-led leadership and empowering people to make their own decisions.

This nontraditional approach to leading and working clearly went against the grain of the traditional hierarchical structure of business. I wanted to disrupt this traditional approach because I found it to be disengaging and lacking in heart.

I also knew there was risk involved. I didn't know if everyone at the organization would like this new approach or if some people would leave the company because of it. I knew that mistakes were going to be made while we integrated Bold Kindness into our culture and shifted the way we worked and led. It took time to successfully integrate an approach where we were all speaking the same language.

Years later, we have established a culture we are so proud of. In taking a chance and embracing being uncomfortable, we transformed everything about who we are, how we work and how we cultivate our team members.

The truth is that disruption requires change, and change can be uncomfortable. In making this change, we disrupted our norm and created a level of discomfort for us as leaders and for our teams as well. We shifted from a mediocre mindset to a performance-accelerating mindset, and this shift required belief.

To be frank, this mindset is not for everyone. I knew that when I asked the leadership team to step into this with me. Some of them believed in it and in its potential impact. Those people stayed. Other people weren't aligned with it, and they didn't remain with us. There are always going to be people who don't want to disrupt their lives; they like being told what to do and keeping things the way they are. Challenging that takes belief, persistence and patience.

Arif's story

Arif, our Vice President, Global Franchise Development, had been working with Nurse Next Door for eight years before I joined the company and began introducing Bold Kindness. He openly shared his struggles with the transition and how he almost left Nurse Next Door because of it.

"When a company evolves their culture or transitions to a new philosophy, it can be very difficult for people who are used to a certain way of working," Arif told me. "And that included me." He noted that when we first talked about moving to a performance-accelerating mindset, he initially saw it as a challenge to him. "I didn't like being questioned about the work I had done or the results I had driven," Arif said. "I felt like it was a challenge of what I had achieved. I took it personally, so personally that it got to the point where I was ready to leave."

Fortunately for our business, Arif didn't leave. He and I sat on the couch together and had a very real and genuine conversation about what I expected, where the possibilities lay and how we could challenge the industry. Arif shared: "I remember realizing that perhaps you were challenging me because you believed in the results I could achieve, and in the results we could all achieve. I realized that perhaps you were challenging me because you care. And I saw that I needed to evolve my own perception of things and be open to being challenged. I needed to be open to Bold Kindness."

Since that conversation, Arif has had the opportunity to lead us into hundreds of new markets, launch internationally and achieve results no one else in the industry has been able to achieve. He has received numerous personal and professional awards due to those results. And I believe that much of that is because he was willing to embrace being uncomfortable and challenge the norm of what he thought.

The expectations I believed he could deliver eight years ago are now the same expectations he has of his team: achieving and unlocking potential in the business and in themselves.

Embedding a disruptive mindset

Here's the important thing: *Disruption has to be embedded in our mindset as leaders.* This is a huge distinction. It's not a one-and-done deal. For me, it's continuously thinking about business from a performance-accelerating mindset. Where can I improve the business? How can I avoid the status quo? What's wildly possible, in both myself and the company I am running?

To create great things, I have to mindfully stay in that place, every day, where I might be on the edge of something great. I have to be unafraid of making mistakes. I have to constantly be thinking: *How can I disrupt the market, myself and my team?*

However, performance acceleration isn't about disrupting the mindset without intention. It's not about forging ahead without considering the outcome or whom I'm going to affect. It's not about showing off or shaking up the market just for the heck of it.

Leaders play a key role in making sure an organization reaps the benefits of disruption without suffering from the potential chaos and loss of energy it can produce. The following themes are what I focus on to find the right balance between disruption and continuity.

Aligning disruption with purpose

When they founded Nurse Next Door, Ken and John picked bright pink and yellow as their brand colors. I love that. I think it symbolizes how disruptive they were in their thinking back then. We continue to evolve that spirit, whether it's through our bold brand colors and advertising or our leadership and culture philosophy.

We didn't just randomly decide to be disruptive to shake things up or get people talking about us. The decision to forge our brand identity was rooted in our take on who our customers are and where they are usually at, emotionally and psychologically, when it comes time to consider home care.

Every innovative idea needs to align with our purpose and drive results. Here's an example. At Nurse Next Door, we disrupt the market through our care philosophy of Happier Aging and the belief that seniors can stay at home. In one radio spot, I bluntly addressed seniors and talked about how no one wants to live in a retirement facility. This *really* got attention. We received letters from retirement facilities, seniors' associations and family members who were outraged by the ad. There was a lot of emotional conversation about how it made them feel. The intent was to spark a conversation about challenging the norms that exist in the industry and in our lives.

The radio ad initiative aligned with our purpose: to disrupt the industry, make lives better through Happier Aging and provide more choice for seniors to age at home. Had the radio ad *not* aligned, it would have been my job as a leader to quash the effort.

The courage to be disruptive

When I think about the biggest learnings I've had at Nurse Next Door, they have to do with being too tolerant and not holding the culture to the highest expectations. At one time, I let the culture get a little vanilla. I let our team walk by little things that, over time, turned into larger cultural shifts. When I look back on that, I realize I questioned my own confidence and belief and whether what I was doing was right or wrong. I went to a place of scarcity.

For instance, I recall having an issue with another leadership team member. We had differing views on a key area of growth for the company. I wanted to implement processes that would bring franchises more in line with our culture; this team member had very strong feelings about doing it another way. I ended up questioning my own inclinations and went with their recommendation. I didn't come out and talk about it. I hid it away. My confidence eroded, and I didn't boldly move forward and make the disruptive changes that were needed. As a result, we continued to be inconsistent with our approach to things and unintentionally kept operating in silos. We had the best intentions, but we stayed stuck in a mediocre place because we couldn't move forward to focus on improving what we needed to.

I remember doing a lot of soul-searching about the issue and really examining what I was doing as the President & CEO of the company. It was a self-exploration in which I asked myself how I needed to evolve and believe even more strongly in myself. It was a journey of being radically honest with myself. I needed to step into the belief that Nurse Next Door does great things and has a great culture and that I needed to help us do more of that. That means saying no when I believe it is necessary or saying yes when no one else wants to.

I feel like when I first started with Nurse Next Door, I was just dabbling in what it was like to be disruptive. And now I love it. I'm bold with it. I'm unapologetic. I get that it's different and that it's not typical. I want this organization to care yet be unapologetic for what we do and how we do it.

The courage to be disruptive has to come from leaders; otherwise, it's not going to work. How I show up is how others are going to show up. Whether your company has a single owner or a board of directors, they have to have your back. I would never be able to do what I do if it weren't for the support of Ken Sim, our owner. He believes in what I'm doing, and he gives me the space to take chances.

Challenging the stories we tell ourselves

When you think about it, we tell ourselves stories all day long. Things like, *We've always done it like this*, or *I need more team members to do the work, and there aren't enough people applying for jobs.* The thing is, these are stories without solutions. We may think there is no way to get around something and even be convinced it's true. Disruption requires us to challenge the stories that don't work for us and tell that story in a different way.

Instead of thinking, *We've always done it like this*, I ask myself, *I wonder if there's a better way I haven't thought of?* Instead of declaring that it's hard to find people, I might think, *I'm working on finding a solution to my people challenge, and maybe I need to ask for help.* Words matter. When I tell myself how things are and stay fixed in a story, I shut down possibilities.

Staying calm

It's really hard to be disruptive if I'm wrapped up in some drama. It's only by staying calm in my approach that I can clearly navigate a situation. So yes, sometimes I'll get really excited about an idea because I see the potential for where it can go. And I know I also have to approach it calmly and with purpose. I might need to step away, to sit with myself or to go for a run. I generate calm by not rushing into a decision. When I do that, I can anticipate obstacles (well, most of them) and move forward in the most deliberate way possible.

It's difficult to make decisions when I have too much going on in my brain or I'm too busy or stressed about something. I can overreact to a situation. I need to spend time with a thought, without overthinking it. Let it sit. Even if I'm feeling unsure or scared about what I'm doing, I try to take my time. To move fast, I have to start slowly.

Being persuasive, not pushy

I feel like I'm stating the obvious here. I think we're past this idea that you have to be a jerk or a bully to disrupt the market and be successful. I don't believe people resonate with that style anymore. (Did they ever?) Quite frankly, people are tired of putting up with that type of thing. Whether it's due to the pandemic or social movements that are happening around the world, people aren't interested in having someone else's power projected on them or in being preached to. I get far more out of people if I remain open, vulnerable and honest with my ideas and stay curious. That's what inspires me—and them.

BOLD KIND REFLECTIONS: DISRUPTING WITH INTENTION

- What does disruption feel like to you?
- Where do you need to challenge the status quo in your life?
- If you knew you couldn't fail, what would you do?

Focus and Flexibility

At first glance, when I talk about purpose and disruption, it may sound like I'm mixing apples and oranges. After all, clarifying purpose is a way to maintain stability in an organization; disruption is about change. The fact is that disruption adds value *only* if it helps an organization achieve its purpose in new and innovative ways. Otherwise, you may find yourself quickly off track. That's why you have to commit to both clarity of purpose *and* disruption. Doing so will allow you to provide guidance so your organization can move in a Bolder Kinder direction without losing focus on why you exist in the first place.

PART 3
———

BOLD KIND
CULTURE

Business is *people*. It doesn't matter *what* kind of business we have or what type of industry we're in. We can have great strategies, a solid business plan and a lean organization. We can have all of the systems and processes we think we need. However, we are not going to excel unless our team members are valued and cared for and are able to grow and succeed in their roles. If we're not building a culture of people development and engagement, we will remain mediocre and get mediocre results.

The thing is, people know when they're valued and when they're not. They know when their leaders believe in them and when they don't. They know when we're going through the motions: when we're giving performance reviews and just ticking off the boxes without truly considering them as people. And they will likely go along with such mediocre treatment, nod their heads, listen to the performance reviews, and perhaps they will marginally improve their performance. They might even do a good job and stay with the company for a while. However, they won't be truly engaged or deliver their best work.

Instead, they will simply look forward to the end of the day, to the end of the week, to work being over. You just have to listen to the radio. Radio hosts routinely say things like, "Only two more days until the weekend." And I think, Is someone's work week really so awful that they need to celebrate every time they get a break from it? How crazy is it that we're living in a world where everyone thinks that's normal? We're spending much of our lives at work, and we're so unhappy when it's only Wednesday and we want the week to end.

If people felt valued and cared for in their work, would they still want to escape it? Can you imagine how it would be if people were excited to come to work on Monday?

We need to create a culture where that can happen. If we want people to be engaged and do a great job, we have to sincerely care about who they are. We need to show up for our team members and support their learning and growth beyond traditional people engagement and performance management strategies. I believe we need to take a long, hard look at how we care about people, how we enable them to be the best version of themselves and how we create a team that is unafraid to roll up their sleeves, make mistakes and get stuff done.

This is where a Bold Kind culture comes in. A Bold Kind culture is a people development culture: one in which team members are kind, caring, self-led and empowered to bring their full, authentic selves to work. It's an environment in which people love coming to work and are valued for their contributions. A Bold Kind culture is generated by leaders who mentor and care for team members and support them in continuously finding better ways of doing things.

By boldly caring for our people and mentoring (not managing) them, we can help create an environment for them to be the best, most authentic versions of themselves. Bold Kind people work as One Team that is focused on Continuous Improvement. They aren't afraid of speaking their truth and making mistakes in their efforts to find a better way.

In the chapters that follow, I outline the Bold Kind people practices we believe in and use every day. This is how we work at Nurse Next Door. Over time, these practices have radically changed our culture and organizational structure, increased engagement and directly contributed to the company's business and financial growth.

There are several key components to building a culture of Bold Kindness, all of which are codependent on one another:

- A Caring Foundation: Creating a foundation of caring team members—through Bold Hiring and people development practices—who believe in a culture of care

- Cultivating Self-Led Leaders: Ensuring all team members are empowered to take personal responsibility for their work and lives

- Abundance Mindset: Encouraging our team to be open to growth and possibilities and engage in a mindset of Continuous Improvement

- REAL Conversations: Having open, honest and caring dialogue with team members and showing up as our full selves in every interaction with them

- Mentoring, Not Managing: Leading teams in a way that provides them with the *what*, not the *how*

Your business environment and approach to culture will undoubtedly be different from Nurse Next Door's, and I encourage you to be curious. Curious about how you can shift your culture to one in which your people love coming to work, especially on Mondays. Curious about how your organization shows their team members they care. Curious about how you lead. Curious about cultivating team members who openly share their passions and who support you and your company in achieving your shared goals.

CHAPTER 7

A CARING FOUNDATION

A few years back, an influential new team member joined Nurse Next Door. They had great skills and wonderful ideas. They were exactly what we needed! And at first we thought it was going to work out well. This individual seemed like they were a good fit. They were driven to improve our systems and processes and brought boldness to the organization.

After a while, something shifted. This individual had a working style that, over time, became less people-oriented and more transactional. Our culture started to change as a result. Team members weren't showing the same level of care, kindness and thoughtfulness in their interactions. The work became a series of tasks, and there was a lack of care in what we were doing and how we were showing up in some departments. We stopped putting people first in how we worked and interacted.

The issue wasn't apparent right away; it happened gradually, day by day. Our company was expanding, and we thought these culture changes and growing pains were "normal." We figured it was just part of the process. Looking back on it now, though, I see that we didn't follow our instincts, which told us something didn't feel right.

At a certain point, we realized our culture and people practices had shifted to a different place. The shift really impacted the entire organization, and some people ended up leaving as a result of their experience. It took us a year to reset our culture to what it was meant to be and to redefine to our people how, first and foremost, we lead with care.

Our leadership team learned something very valuable from this experience. Regardless of how big we became, it was important to never lose our humanity and to never bend the culture. We drifted off course because we didn't stay true to our culture. We made erroneous assumptions that everything was okay. It wasn't.

Even if someone has the skills and experience to elevate the way we work, it won't work if it's not a good fit or if they try to change who we are. We are, first and foremost, a people development organization, and that means putting people *first*.

We have since honed our approach to ensure we have *a caring foundation of team members who believe in what we're doing*. This approach has two components: Bold Hiring and Living the Culture. Bold Hiring is about ensuring we have the right people on board from the get-go. We have elevated our Bold Hiring practices to ensure we are hiring self-led people who are committed to our purpose and who believe in our values and how we work. For us, ensuring someone is a good fit is even more important than their skill set. We also focus on Living the Culture: ensuring our purpose and culture are always at the forefront of our efforts and guide everything we do.

Bold Hiring

At Nurse Next Door, we have built a Bold Kind culture of self-led leaders who take responsibility for their own success and approach their work with an Abundance Mindset. In the next chapter, I get more into self-led leaders—who they are, why they are important and how to cultivate them. To develop such an amazing, caring team, we had to start at the very beginning: hiring the right people in the first place.

Through Bold Hiring, we disrupt the traditional model of hiring people by boldly caring about our team members and being committed to their development and success. We are interested in the *person*, not just what's on their resume.

I'll give you an example. I remember we were hiring for a role, and we had two final candidates. Let's call them Jana and Marta. Jana was very polished and confident, had an amazing resume, and presented herself beautifully. We felt 100 percent certain she could do the job. Marta, to be honest, didn't conduct her interview as well. She was somewhat shy and self-effacing. She also didn't have much experience in her role.

Of course, most companies would automatically hire Jana. She was clearly the stronger choice. And we hired Marta. Here's why. She was a kind person. She was nice to be around and loved our culture. And she was keen to learn and grow. We instinctively felt that even though she wasn't as polished, she connected with us, and we connected with her. It came down to us asking our team who they thought would be the better fit. Our team unequivocally said it should be Marta. So we hired her, and we've never regretted it. We've supported her in developing her skill set, and she is thriving in her role. She has been an amazing contributor to our team.

While skills are very important to us, we're actually more interested in finding people who are going to fit with our culture, care for others and have integrity about what they do. We take chances on people who may otherwise be overlooked. We don't want someone who thinks they have all the answers. We are looking for Bold Kind people who bring a fresh perspective and approach and are curious about how they can learn and grow. We're looking for people we can form caring relationships with and support them in their journey.

We have found that when we welcome team members who love our culture and are passionate about it, they will thrive, even if they don't have as much experience as someone else. We work with them to develop any needed skills, which generally results in them excelling and making tremendous contributions. We want people who are in alignment with our culture and who can personally thrive and grow with us.

As I state earlier, even though we want people to align with our culture, what's as important is that they *belong to themselves* and can show up 100 percent for themselves. They need to feel a sense of personal connection to the company and how we fit in with their overall life goals, regardless of how long they stay with us.

Hiring people who align with our culture isn't always easy. We've learned not to rush the process. For instance, I recall one time when we were in a hurry to find someone, as we had a pressing need to fill that role. We had interviewed a number of individuals already, and we were at a point where we found someone whose skill set looked amazing. We could see they would bring much-needed talent to the table (much like the example with Jana above). Because we were in a hurry to hire someone, we rushed the interview process, particularly some of the details around culture and how we worked, and hired the individual.

After working with this individual for a short while, it was evident that they assumed we had already built certain processes and systems, which they would be able to follow. We actually needed someone to build the process *for* us. We needed someone who was going to be nimble and curious and help us learn and grow. They wanted a role where they could follow the process and wanted things to be very black and white. So ultimately this individual didn't work out. Even if someone is very qualified, they won't thrive if they are not fully on board with our culture, which includes a strong focus on Continuous Improvement and finding a better way.

We also realized that we have to hire people who are confident in themselves and their own beliefs and can let us know early on when their values and approaches aren't in alignment with Nurse Next Door's. We can't force someone to love a culture or believe in our beliefs—they have to *want* to.

Based on this experience, we spent a lot of time reflecting on this hire and our process, including what we learned and what we would do differently next time. And that work continues to this day. We continue to reflect and evolve our processes to clearly communicate who we are and what we believe in. We want to ensure a potential candidate understands how we work and wants to sign up for it.

A FOUNDATION OF
PEOPLE DEVELOPMENT

A Bold Kind culture is not possible unless your company is rooted in meaningful people commitments that capture your culture of care and focus on people development. Having written people commitments helps demonstrate to your team members that you truly care about them and are invested in their happiness and success. They also help keep your team accountable for living and breathing the culture.

PEOPLE PROMISE

At Nurse Next Door, our commitment to team members starts with our People Promise. It's our goal to shift the perception of caregiving. We believe it should be a noble and rewarding career—one to aspire to. To support that, we have been leading the charge and establishing ourselves as the career destination of choice. We provide growth opportunities and guaranteed hours. Our culture and employment practices attract the most caring and dedicated caregivers. We provide for our people so they feel fulfilled in their jobs. We treat our caregivers with respect and help them achieve their dreams and goals. By being kind to our people and spending time developing them, we have brought professionalism to the industry.

Our People Promise is our employee brand differentiator and sets us apart from our competitors. We communicate it to all prospective team members to let them know we care about them and are invested in their success.

OUR PEOPLE PROMISE

You love coming to work.

You are treated with kindness and have found belonging at Nurse Next Door. You have strong relationships with your clients, team members and leader. You are committed to your job and have flexibility in how you manage your time. You see the possibility of caregiving as a career, and your leader is helping you achieve this.

You are appreciated for the work you put in and given the freedom to care for your clients the way you would care for your mom or dad. You feel engaged and want to make lives better—and you're having fun along the way.

CULTURE DECK

To deepen our commitment, we also created a Nurse Next Door Culture Deck. This clearly and simply outlines our Bold Kind culture, including our beliefs, commitment of care to our team members and expectations of our people. It includes our Values, People Promise, people development practices and the principles that guide us along our way.

By having a Culture Deck, we clearly lay everything out on the table. This way, prospective team members can immediately understand what's important to us and decide if they want to be a part of that. A Culture Deck is also a great litmus test to help weed out people who aren't a good fit for our organization.

We state it pretty clearly in the deck: "We get it. Our Bold Kindness approach might not suit you. It's pretty radical, and if you're not on board with it, no problem. Just let us know now, and we'll warmly encourage you on your

continued

journey elsewhere. If you are into it, and if you feel like the idea of Making Lives Better pulls at something deep and essential within your soul, we're thrilled. We only ask that you embrace it wholeheartedly and without apology."

YOUR PEOPLE COMMITMENTS

When you look at your people commitments, ask yourself: *Do they excite people? Do they demonstrate care for my team members? Are they meaningful and relevant to our organizational goals?* If not, I encourage you to get curious about your commitments and start a conversation with your team to challenge your current state. Having meaningful, authentic people commitments are key to driving a Bold Kind culture.

The first conversations

All of this starts with the first conversations we have with a prospective team member.

When we first meet someone, we don't follow a formal or rigid approach in which we immediately question them about their experiences and skills. We want to get to know them and to build a meaningful relationship with prospective team members from the get-go. So yes, we will talk about their skills and their current role, and more than that, we address their whole person. We want to know their likes and dislikes. We want to know what makes them happy and where they are challenged. We bring in other team members to meet potential newcomers and share their opinions on what this person will bring to the team and where they may potentially need support.

These first conversations do require an investment of time, and it's worth it. I get more into this in the later chapter on REAL Conversations. We believe that every conversation presents an opportunity to get to know someone better and deepen our relationship with them.

Alignment with core values

As part of those first conversations, we not only want to get to know someone, we also want to know if they align with our culture and core values. Our core values—*Admire people, WOW customer experience, Find a better way* and *Passionate about making a difference*—drive every decision in our organization.

- **Admire people:** Our clients aren't just case files; they're real people. We admire everyone and treat them with respect: our clients, their families, our team members and everyone we meet.

  We look for team members who are kind and considerate of clients and fellow team members. How do they speak to other people? How do they talk about their friends or former colleagues?

- **WOW customer experience:** "Good" just won't do. We show a caring attitude, anticipate future needs and inspire confidence. We are clear, honest and prompt in our communication. We don't rest until we've exceeded expectations and wowed customers with our compassion and service.

When we interview candidates, we look for people who care about others. In what ways have they helped team members, clients and friends? What is their communication style? Are they happy with a satisfactory resolution, or do they strive to go above and beyond?

- **Find a better way:** We promote an entrepreneurial culture where creativity, individual initiative and out-of-the-box thinking is the norm. We embrace the spirit of Continuous Improvement and always search for a better way to provide our services.

  We look for people who want to work for and contribute to an organization that is innovative, positive and future-focused. Do they work well with others? Do they search for better, more efficient ways of doing things?

- **Passionate about making a difference:** We look for people who genuinely care about what they're doing and strive to do things for the common good. We work together as a team, to innovate and grow, and make a real difference in people's lives.

  They want to work for us because they have a deep-seated desire to help others. Are they kind? Do they express care for people in their community?

To further align with our culture, we look for candidates with these additional attributes:

- Authenticity: They are genuine in who they are. They don't try to conform to a certain type of person that "fits the role." They bring their true self (even if it's less polished around the edges) and authentically interact with us. We go past the resume and look at the person.

- Self-led critical thinker: They come from a place of abundance and see possibility. They have experiences (e.g., education, work, sports, activities) that help them call on critical thinking skills. They can independently raise awareness of issues and opportunities and bring forward solutions.

- Skills: Their skills (education, experience and attitude) go beyond the needs of the role. They are interested in growing and expanding their talents and challenging themselves beyond the immediate needs of their job.

Topgrading

Once we feel strongly that a candidate is right for us, we use topgrading behavioral interviews. This hiring and interview methodology, which was developed by Bradford D. Smart, helps us verify candidates share our culture and values and determine the consistency of their character across a range of situations. It helps us understand a candidate's past education and work to determine if they are well-suited to Nurse Next Door's culture and the available position. Topgrading enables us to see patterns and trends in a candidate's life, from what they were like in high school to any difficulties they had to overcome in their life. We believe that past performance determines future performance.

Topgrading also gives us an opportunity to further our relationship with them. By having them be open, honest and transparent about their experiences, we can deepen our connections with them. We typically spend two hours on the final topgrading interview; we feel it's important to dedicate that time to people we are serious about. Candidates frequently comment on how they enjoyed the opportunity to reflect on their previous experience and feel this is a miss in other organizations.

Living the Culture

Once we have hired a new team member, it doesn't stop there. We make a point of ensuring all of our team members live and embrace our culture on an ongoing basis. That means defining the culture, then consistently generating it.

Our definition of culture starts with our purpose: Making Lives Better. I elaborate on this in chapter 2. Our company exists to Make Lives Better—for our clients, our team members and everyone we meet. This is the first step in having a Bold Kind culture of care. We support that with our core philosophy of Happier Aging in which we help people find joy and happiness, regardless of what stage of life they're at.

Vision

A vision statement is such a powerful tool for expressing an organization's meaning and purpose. Thing is, we wanted more than a vision statement. We wanted to visualize and articulate where we want our company to go in the future and to fully express our Bold Kind culture and commitment to care.

As a result, our team created a Painted Picture. The Painted Picture articulates our vision and culture by outlining our goals over an eighteen-month period. When we keep our team in the loop about the organization, including our dreams and how we want to show up in the world, we empower our team members to feel a sense of belonging and care. Our Painted Picture is clear, simple and direct. We make sure to keep it updated so that we are always growing and moving forward and ensure our team is crystal clear on our objectives. We also ensure we align our daily operations and actions with the larger vision; everything we do is intended to drive the goals in our Painted Picture.

Communicating vision and purpose

It's not enough to create a purpose or vision statement and set of values, post them on our website or put them in an employee handbook, then never talk about them again. That's a missed opportunity. We need to create space to live and breathe the culture.

All of us leaders at Nurse Next Door make sure we are crystal clear in communicating our vision to our team members and making sure they're on board. After all, it's not only critical for us as leaders to maintain, grow and respect a company's purpose and vision, it's also equally important for our team members to do the same. If we can't clearly share with our team where the company is going, they will have trouble connecting their day-to-day work with the bigger vision and objectives. Also, if our team members don't believe in what the company is doing, they're not going to be the best version of themselves.

When we first launch a new Painted Picture every eighteen months, we communicate it to all team members via our weekly huddles and check-ins. More importantly, we live it. By ensuring all of our actions align with our goals, and setting an example of a culture of care, we inspire others to do the same.

When our team members fall in love with the vision and purpose, they are more passionate because they can see their work makes a difference. Our Painted Picture allows everyone to see themselves living our purpose (Making Lives Better) and it connects the tactical everyday work to the larger strategic initiatives. It's what motivates them to show up for themselves and others and can bring personal joy and happiness to their lives. Our culture also has to align with how they find meaning in their own lives—I speak more to that in a bit.

Staying true to culture

You might recall the story from an earlier chapter about how when I started at Nurse Next Door, people rarely did the dishes. Instead of being judgmental about the dirty dishes, I used my curiosity to work with my fellow leaders to identify *why* it was happening and what it would take to change the situation.

As I mention earlier, someone else might not worry about a dirty dish in the sink. It is a small and simple act. What is one dirty cup, dish or plate? It's the small acts, though, that teach us the most about behavior. Small acts can also add up to something much bigger and more significant. How we do anything is how we do everything. And what we realized over time is that people who left dirty dishes in the sink or did not tidy up after themselves in communal areas were not taking whole-hearted responsibility for their actions. If they weren't taking whole-hearted responsibility for something as simple as a dish, how else did that manifest in their work and lives? And how could we, as a company, stay agile and forward-moving if our team wasn't taking responsibility for everything they did?

So I sat down with the leadership team and we talked about it. We peeled back the layers of engagement and explored them further. We knew we had to do something different. We had to change the feeling and culture of the team and encourage a culture of self-led leadership. We also knew that, if we expected others to do the dishes, we had to do them ourselves and leave things better than we found them.

This was about more than just doing the dishes. We wanted to empower our team to make decisions and to be accountable for their every action, no matter how big or small. Every decision, conversation, meeting we attend or don't attend, questions we answer or don't answer . . . they all matter when it comes to generating culture.

That's why we don't bend when it comes to culture. We learned not to walk by something that wasn't aligned with who we are. Ignoring the seemingly small stuff—dirty dishes, someone not showing up to work on time, the conversation that needs to be had—has a negative impact. So that means smiling when someone walks in the door. Looking them in the eye. Following up on a task. Cleaning your mug after you've used it. Having that hard conversation. Treating others with respect and care.

Responsibilities beyond job descriptions

If someone at Nurse Next Door says something is not in their job description, that's a pretty good indication they're not a good fit for our culture. We don't operate in boxes.

That's not to say people should do things that are wildly outside of their skill set: A graphic designer is not expected to work in franchise development, and an analytics specialist shouldn't be creating profit-and-loss statements. However, all of us make the best contribution when we are curious about and aware of what is happening around us and speak up if we see there may be a better way of doing something. For instance, a team member might be invited to a meeting related to a project they're not working on, or a topic that's outside their area of expertise. We want to get their perspective as an outsider and even to poke holes in what is being done. We find this can provide a fresh point of view on what we are doing and keep us on our toes.

If people operate solely in assigned roles, a job becomes more about protecting and staying within one's department, rather than driving results and contributing to the company's purpose. In my experience, when we get attached to job titles and responsibilities, nothing good comes from that. It restricts us.

When we're excited about work and people, and working collaboratively, that's when it's awesome. And yes, I think it's important to have clarity about roles and what people are doing. There also needs to be fluidity. We welcome and encourage curiosity and interdepartmental collaboration to find solutions. There is no hard line for problem-solving at Nurse Next Door. We only win when we *all* win.

One Best Way to live our purpose and culture

When Nurse Next Door started, it was very much an entrepreneurially run organization. I joke about this, and I always say that when I started here, we had eighty versions of what a good job looks like. Every franchisee had a different way of doing things, and there was little to no standardization. And because we had so many ways of doing things, we didn't have one way that reflected who we are.

As a result, our culture and brand were interpreted in many different ways. This was not only inefficient and ineffective, but it also meant we weren't all living a Bold Kind culture. So we had to get a handle on that. We needed systems and processes that could help us scale and grow, while still staying nimble and true to our culture.

As a result, we introduced One Best Way: the systems and processes we created to embed our culture across the organization. It includes everything from onboarding franchisees to conducting intakes (the initial phone call with a client) and consults (the sales process), all the way to client visits and how we work with one another. These aren't arbitrary systems and processes. We created and honed them over the span of many years, trying out different approaches and practices until we found what works the best and what helps us stay true to our purpose and culture.

By following One Best Way, we ensure our workflow processes and practices are aligned to our purpose and culture and consistently adhered to without inefficient work-arounds, one-offs or Band-Aid solutions. It ensures we are able to help our franchisees grow their businesses in the most effective way and align with our care philosophy of Happier Aging.

To accomplish One Best Way, all of our team members must all work together and be aligned in following our processes and practices. We believe that when we all work together, we get the best results for each other. We make a point of establishing culture and One Best Way at the very start of every relationship with a franchisee or team member. That helps everyone fully align with the culture and keep it alive.

Keeping culture in the foreground

Culture must be omnipresent, from the very first interaction with a potential team member to day-to-day interactions. When team members are not living the culture on a regular basis, everyone notices. When people are hierarchical, unkind or uncaring, it impacts the way everyone works. When they bring their full, caring selves to each and every moment, it trickles down throughout the organization.

By embedding Bold Hiring practices, including who you bring on, how you bring them on and how you set them up, you can lay a Bold Kind foundation in which team members are cared for and believe in what you're doing.

This focus on culture needs to continue as your business expands (*especially* as your business expands). What are the non-negotiables? What are you unwilling to compromise on?

Staying true to culture can be a real challenge, and meeting that challenge is what can be so fun: figuring out ways to bring your company forward while staying true to your roots. You do it by making culture an active, living, breathing part of everything you do. That provides a path for moving forward.

In subsequent chapters I get into the ways in which we live our culture and develop our team members by Cultivating Self-Led Leaders, promoting an Abundance Mindset, having REAL Conversations, and Mentoring, Not Managing.

BOLD KIND REFLECTIONS: A CARING FOUNDATION

- What does kindness feel like to you?
- What is one thing you can do today to stretch your heart wider?
- How do you allow others to shine?
- What are your daily practices to show your team kindness and care?

CHAPTER 8

CULTIVATING
SELF-LED LEADERS

T hroughout this book I reference self-led leaders: team members who guide their own success and take responsibility for their actions. Because self-led leadership is such an incredibly important part of a Bold Kind culture, I'd like to spend more time on it in this chapter.

Self-led leaders are team members who are empowered to lead themselves and take responsibility for their own actions. Self-led leaders are able to guide themselves toward a desired outcome, instead of relying on others to tell them what to do. They are also self-aware and have the emotional intelligence to know how they're showing up and how to self-regulate if their emotions run high. They're clear on who they are and what they want. They respond instead of reacting. Most of all, self-led leaders are curious: They take the initiative and are lifelong learners who are constantly seeking a way to be and do better. They take responsibility for what they do and make decisions about how to achieve goals.

At Nurse Next Door, self-led leadership doesn't mean people work in silos or make decisions independently from their teams. It means they are welcomed and encouraged to take a seat at the table and bring solutions, contribute to goals and drive results in the organization without fear of being reprimanded for stepping on someone's toes.

In my experience, people don't want to be managed or put in a box. They want to have options and the choice to decide how they're going to do something.

Here's an example. In a traditional workplace, a leader might tell their sales team that sales are down and dictate specific actions that need to be done: make more calls to potential clients, increase field visits, etc.

In a self-led environment, the team takes initiative and notices that sales are down, without waiting for someone to call it to their attention and require action. They get curious about how to approach the problem and discuss it as a team. They come up with solutions to increase sales. They inform their leader of their proposed plan and seek advice where needed. Then they work together to take action. In this way, they have the freedom and autonomy to come up with solutions on their own and make a more meaningful contribution. They own their results: both the successes and the failures.

At Nurse Next Door, self-led leadership is a way to actively embrace one of our Happier Aging principles—Autonomy— which is the right to make decisions for ourselves, free of outside influences. We know that we may not control life's circumstances, and being the authors of our lives means deciding what we do with them. We want our people to be in charge of their own professional paths and to support them along the way. Someone's tenure at the organization is irrelevant. It's all about their desire to learn, improve and grow.

As self-led leaders, our team members are always pushing themselves to do better and continue to wow us with their creativity and ingenuity. To provide them with the space to lead and be independent, we give them control over how they do their work. They are empowered to make decisions. Their opinions are valued and listened to. We're clear on the goal, and we allow them to figure it out from there. We trust our teams to implement the best processes and to create a place where people can make mistakes. We see mistakes as opportunities to learn and grow, and we are not judgmental. I get more into this in subsequent chapters.

I believe that you can create an *environment* for a self-led leader; you can't *create* a self-led leader. Self-led leaders have this characteristic built into them; they are driven to do better and be better.

Having said that, being a self-led leader takes work. It requires time and personal investment. It takes confidence, curiosity and vulnerability. Self-led leaders are open to making mistakes and learning to do better. Self-led leadership doesn't work well for people who want to protect their job stability, "just want to do their job" or aren't open to feedback. And you're going to find there are some people in your organization who don't want to be self-led and who are happy having middle managers and being told what to do. This is why, as I talk about in the previous chapter, it's essential to use Bold Hiring practices to bring on self-led leaders who align with your culture.

I do believe that self-led leaders can be inspired and challenged in lots of ways. For instance, I like to come up with fun goals for our franchise development team. Once I said, "How about ten for ten? If you bring in ten new franchises in February, you'll each get ten thousand dollars." Now, someone who's not a self-led leader might think, *Ten new partners in one month? That's impossible.* We have people in franchise development who are curious and driven, and they got excited about the challenge and made it work. You find that everywhere at Nurse Next Door.

Let's get into some other ways we inspire self-led leaders and create an environment for them to thrive at Nurse Next Door.

Bold Dreams and Bold Goals

Self-led leaders are far more effective when they are clear on what they want and the steps needed to take them there. That's why we encourage everyone across the organization to design a life they love by pursuing their passions and aspirations. This is what we call Bold Dreams and Bold Goals (BDBGs). We use our BDBG program to help our team members home in on what they really care about and want to achieve. We define Bold as courageous, up for the challenge and willing to go against the status quo.

A Bold Dream is what we create when we get clear about what we want our life to look and feel like in the future. It can relate to any aspect of our lives, whether it's a career aspiration or a personal goal. Dreams are the foundation of what will become our reality. We encourage each other, as well as our caregivers and clients, to discover their dreams by visualizing themselves in the future and asking themselves questions such as:

- What drives and excites you?
- What experiences do you want to have?
- How do you want to feel?
- What kind of life do you want to live?

The next step is to put plans in place—Bold Goals—for achieving the Bold Dream. The Bold Goals describe how the person will actualize their dreams. Bold Goals should be SMART: specific, measurable, achievable, relevant and time-bound. Some examples of Bold Goals might be:

- I am going to attend three fitness classes this week to achieve my wellness goal.
- I am going to save $10,000 by December 31 toward the purchase of a car.
- I am going to sign up for and complete a course in French by next March.

We really care about our team members and want to hear about what's important to them. That's why we host a Bold Dreams Bold Goals session twice every year. Team members are encouraged to create a Bold Dream to get clear about what they want their life and work to look like in the future. They can also articulate their Bold Goals, which is how they will actualize their dream and make it a reality. Team members are encouraged to share their personal dreams with us so we can cheer them on and celebrate when they achieve personal and professional milestones.

LETTING PEOPLE GO THEIR OWN WAY

It's important to note that someone's dreams might mean they want to explore other opportunities outside of Nurse Next Door and may not stay with us for years. We will still provide them with development and support to help them take on their next goal on the way to achieving their life's dreams. People are not going to be with our organization forever! We celebrate them while they're here, and we celebrate them when they go. For instance, we had someone who was with Nurse Next Door for a number of years, and the individual made great contributions. Ultimately one of their Bold Dreams was to have their own business, so that's what they ended up doing.

A company is always going to change and evolve, so we consistently have conversations with people in which we ask if they are still fulfilled in what they're doing. And if they aren't, that's okay. We always help them with their next steps.

If Bold Dreams and Bold Goals don't work for your organization, find other ways of tapping into what your team members want, personally and professionally. When team members feel you care about their lives—their hopes and dreams and who they are as people—they are likely to achieve more, no matter how long they stay with you.

Beyond Performance Reviews

Over the years, there have been many conversations about the pros and cons of performance reviews. Performance reviews can be great for connecting with people and addressing goals and challenges. The argument for eliminating performance reviews is that they're not always effective. They can be stressful for both the manager and the team member, and providing feedback after the fact (three months later) can be ineffective and deter future performance.

While there are different schools of thought in the matter, I strongly feel that there's a middle ground, one that's more natural and intuitive when it comes to having a caring relationship with a fellow team member. At Nurse Next Door, we don't have traditional performance reviews at set times. We create an environment for self-led leaders to be inspired and guided in the moment. We believe in having informal check-ins on a regular basis.

First, we provide in-the-moment feedback. Instead of saving up feedback for annual performance reviews, we discuss issues as soon as they happen. This immediate feedback gives our team members the opportunity to address the situation in the moment and have an open conversation with us about challenges and areas of growth. Every conversation offers us the chance to have a REAL Conversation (more on that later) and show someone we care about who they are and what they are doing.

We have seen how effective it is to give feedback in the moment, instead of waiting several months to let a team member know they could have done better on a project that has long since finished. It gives them the opportunity to reflect, ask questions and see we care about them. They see we want them to grow and evolve their skills and to succeed in their work. They are able to adjust what they are doing and make the necessary changes to improve or thrive in the project. Our goal is for them to walk out of the conversation feeling confident to make the necessary changes, with the tools they need to do the job.

Second, we do quarterly check-ins. Our senior leaders have informal quarterly discussions with their team members that are *not* about monitoring performance. They're about checking in on people to see what they feel good about, what they're working toward, where they feel challenged and how we can support them. In other words, the check-ins are meant to support and empower team members, not assess, judge or rate them.

Third, we have created a culture where our team members know to reach out if they need help; it is an expectation in how we work. A self-led culture doesn't mean that people are left on their own. We encourage people to reach out to each other or a mentor if they don't know what to do or are unclear on where to go. We encourage them to get feedback when they need it. In other words, we make it okay for them to not have the answers.

Finally, we encourage peer-to-peer feedback. We have weekly team meetings in which we review results achieved, including what went well and what we need to focus on in the coming week to drive results. It's an opportunity for peers to provide feedback, challenge one another and celebrate successes.

I've had team members come to me and say, "I'm stuck. I'm working on this project and I just don't know how to approach it." Instead of telling them what to do, I get curious. I ask them questions and provide guidance. "Which part are you stuck on? Where are the opportunities? Which part of this project are you excited about and why?" By getting curious and asking questions, we give people the space to figure it out for themselves.

I believe that by relying less on performance reviews and instead increasing connectedness, communication and feedback, we've created a culture where people aren't surprised by feedback or feel disempowered in their work. By developing people more frequently and helping them improve their skill set and confidence, they are more open to feedback and guidance. They are more productive. They don't wait around for direction; they figure out new ways of doing things. They're much more engaged with who we are as a company and what they need to do to help fulfill our purpose. And I believe that is what Nurse Next Door has created: a real sense that each person owns their results. We all own our performance.

10 Things That Require Zero Talent

While control over decision-making, having Bold Goals and replacing performance reviews with ongoing conversations represent the fullest ideals of self-led leadership, we believe every team member should take responsibility for their own behavior. So at Nurse Next Door, we started working toward self-led leadership with the basics: how people were showing up. For instance, people were often arriving late to meetings. When they did, it was considered acceptable; they were busy, after all. There were other things as well. I remember being on a call with a group of people. One of them was somewhat detached and rude, and nobody said anything. Nobody had the words to say, "Hey, that's not okay."

The thing is, these actually weren't huge things. They happened in the blink of an eye without disrupting the normal course of business. Like the earlier example with the dishes, it's the small things that add up. By having a workplace in which people were allowed to be disengaged or late to meetings, we were promoting a culture without integrity. It also didn't align with our purpose of Making Lives Better; we weren't making lives better for each other.

Around that time, I came across a social media post titled "10 Things That Require Zero Talent." To me, this really resonated because these are skills that people need to have in their daily workplace and are mandatory for a culture of self-led leadership. What's so great and empowering is that the ten things don't require training or management. They simply require a mindset of professionalism and personal accountability. They are skills that anyone can do.

10 THINGS THAT REQUIRE ZERO TALENT

Being on time: Show up promptly to meetings and deadlines, without excuses.	Attitude: Be kind and know everything is possible.
Work ethic: It's all about results and what's driving your work.	Passion: Care deeply.
Completion: It's not done until it's done.	Being coachable: Listen, learn and grow.
Body language: Lean in, smile and say hello.	Doing extra: We're not a 9-5 company.
Energy: Walk quickly and with purpose.	Being prepared: Show up and contribute.

I distributed this list to our team, and we use the ten things as our guiding principles of behavior to this day. It is a simple tool that has proved incredibly helpful in creating a stepping stone to a culture of self-led leadership.

And if these specific ten things don't resonate with you, come up with your own list of basic skills you can use to hold people accountable. Have high expectations of your team: Communicate these expectations early in the relationship and as often as needed. If you don't, they won't. If you settle for mediocrity, you will get mediocre results. Expect excellence.

Embracing Our Full Selves

In part 2, I talk about how important it is for each of us as leaders to embrace our full selves. We are long past the era where work should be formal, or where personal selves aren't allowed to enter the workplace. At Nurse Next Door, we apply the same principle to everyone; it's part of our goal of self-led leadership. Our team members fit into our culture yet are very unique in and of themselves. They are not afraid to be who they are. They have a point of view. They bring their full selves, and they're constantly looking for ways to improve.

To truly understand our teams and see where they can thrive, we have to invite the personal and professional to flourish. We welcome authenticity and respect. We must establish respect and trust with our people and genuinely care about them. Otherwise, a culture of self-led leadership will not thrive.

I believe one of the reasons why self-led leadership works so well at Nurse Next Door is because people come to work with the same respect they carry in their personal lives. Imagine how exhausting it is for people to show up to work every day having to be someone else. For instance, a team member might have a keen sense of humor but holds back at work because they want to be "professional." Or they may be a new dad, exhausted from sleepless nights, and pretend everything is okay because they don't want to appear "weak." How can we expect them to give it their best and connect with our culture—and each other—if they are constantly pretending?

We do it by being real and fully expressed at work, not by being a different person. It's not a complicated formula. It starts by asking how someone is, then truly caring for them by taking the time to listen and hold space for that person if and when they need it. By keeping it simple and honestly caring about each other, we build trusting, meaningful relationships.

Evolution, Not Revolution

Nurse Next Door has, first and foremost, a culture of people development, a key aspect of which is self-led leadership. The move in this direction can take time. Ours took several years to fully implement; it's not easy to shift away from traditional leadership concepts that focus on a hierarchical approach. It takes a while to get people out of that traditional mindset, and it's worth the extra work.

I believe that we are looking at the next evolution of leadership, where people are able to create their own opportunities within an organization, and that the hierarchical approach to leadership is on its way out.

And no, this change doesn't sit well with everyone. The thing is, organizations can't grow at a rapid speed if people are not taking accountability for their actions. We as leaders have to create a culture where people are 100 percent accountable for their work and for pursuing the overall goals of the organization.

BOLD KIND REFLECTIONS: CULTIVATING SELF-LED LEADERS

- How do you instill self-led leadership in your organization?
- How does your team cultivate a self-led culture?
- What is your team enthusiastic to learn?
- How does your team own their behavior and results?

CHAPTER 9

ABUNDANCE MINDSET

W hen I think about abundance, I go to possibilities. This is why an Abundance Mindset is such an essential component of Bold Kindness: It's about being open to growth and possibilities and maintaining an attitude of Continuous Improvement.

Earlier in the book I talk about having an Abundance Mindset in which I encourage business leaders to see things from the perspective of abundance, not scarcity. In this chapter, I'd like to dive more into what an Abundance Mindset means at Nurse Next Door and how we encourage our entire team to think abundantly so that we foster growth and possibilities.

I believe that when you come from a place of possibility, you open the door to opportunity. This has been a key driver in how Nurse Next Door generates results. It is a mindset we believe in and practice every day.

As an example, when we are looking to solve something, I might hear someone use the common phrase, "Well, the problem is . . ." That type of expression can drag us down from the get-go. When we start off by thinking about something as a problem, we get into the mindset that something is wrong.

Instead, we come at it from a philosophy of abundance and Continuous Improvement and take an approach in which there's a fun, exciting challenge to be solved. When we come from a place of abundance, we might start by asking, "What are the opportunities here? How do we improve?" It means wanting to make things great. This may seem like a small thing, but words matter. The stories we tell ourselves matter. This shift in how we talk impacts how we think, how we solve problems and the results we get.

An Abundance Mindset extends to all areas of our organization, from our relationships to the structure of our teams to the way we compensate our people. When we have an Abundance Mindset, we are always innovating and in a state of Continuous Improvement. We promote a sense of openness and trust when working with one another. We keep teams streamlined, so the skills and innovations of our team members can rapidly surface. We are also flexible with job positions: By being fluid and responsive to our team members' skills and aspirations, we can quickly adjust their roles to allow them to use their strengths and shine. Finally, abundance is about treating people well: By having an Abundance Mindset, we pay people well and encourage fun and creativity.

There are several components of an Abundance Mindset, which I get into now.

Continuous Improvement

At Nurse Next Door, we foster growth from a culture of Continuous Improvement in which we are excited to think bold and go after big things each day. It's about looking forward to continuously iterating and understanding what's needed to efficiently shape our future. It's how we lead our teams every day.

Through Continuous Improvement, we are consistently asking ourselves how we can do better. It's about learning and reflecting on what worked and what didn't. Remember the story I told earlier about our franchise development team coming up with solutions to bringing on more franchisees? They consistently tried out new approaches, fine-tuned them and tried them again. Instead of giving up, they kept at it.

Continuous Improvement is about challenging each other. "Is that goal bold enough? Are we working as efficiently as we can?" Part of challenging each other is about challenging our processes. It's easy to get into habits about the way we work. Continuous Improvement is about pausing, asking questions and challenging our own norms: what we are doing, why we are doing it and whether or not it's working.

We may start a project and, at the beginning, have everything mapped out, with a clear design. Once we start working on it, we may discover that it's not going to work the way we envisioned it. So we'll pause and say, "No, we need to go back to the drawing board." It might be easier to overlook this one thing and say, "Oh, we're fine without it." We don't want it to be fine. We want it to be great. Then we take what we learned and apply it to other projects.

Lean Teams

When people come and visit us at Nurse Next Door, they are often amazed at how small and nimble our team is. We also operate our entire Care Services Center (our client services team) and our head office (what we call HeartQuarters) all on one floor, with everybody working side by side. We keep a lean team.

It's great for organizations to scale and expand, but as they do so, they tend to take on more people and processes to help manage this growth. When there are layers and layers of processes, and more hierarchy, organizations can lose the ability to be nimble and actually slow things down. They lose efficiency and don't maximize profitability. There's little accountability and less passion to find solutions. If a team has too many people, especially those who aren't well paid or nurtured, self-led leadership will never work. This is the thing I love about small- to medium-sized companies; they can be so much more agile than their larger counterparts.

To ensure team members can effectively lead themselves, the overall team needs to function in a lean, nimble fashion, with team members who have growth opportunities, are paid well and enjoy what they're doing.

At Nurse Next Door, we changed the way our organization is designed. We created flexible and agile teams that work toward common goals versus people who work in silos and departments. We wanted to get rid of the "that's not my job" attitude.

By having a lean team, we give our self-led leaders space to do their jobs. When there are layers and layers of people and processes, team members don't have the space they need to thrive.

Eliminating Middle Management

When I first started with Nurse Next Door, our Care Services Center was very hierarchical, with layers of specialists and supervisors. As a result, it took a while to get certain tasks done.

For instance, if there was a scheduling challenge, the specialist would email their manager, who would then review the request. The manager had lots of other things to do, so they might not resolve the issue until hours later. This resulted in the caregiver being dissatisfied (they didn't have confirmation of their schedule) and the client being dissatisfied (they didn't know when a caregiver would be showing up). So there was a huge delay on something that was actually simple to take care of.

The other thing we noticed is that middle managers often got too involved in the day-to-day details of how the work was getting done. So their team members were waiting for instructions instead of taking action. This also affected performance because it meant team members didn't have the confidence or critical thinking skills to perform their role to the fullest extent. Middle management was ineffective, slowing down the business and creating a fatter organization. It also took decision-making opportunities away from the front line and removed the chance for our team to grow and learn and be self-led leaders.

Ultimately, we realized that the more we cultivated self-led leaders who take personal and professional accountability and who show up with these skills every day, without excuses, the less we needed middle management. We needed to create an environment where people could be responsible for their own actions (with guidance), and that meant eliminating a layer. It was time to flatten the organization.

So how did we go about eliminating middle management? We started by assessing the current team and roles and having one-on-ones with all team members to discuss their roles, including what was and wasn't working and where the bottlenecks were. We didn't get rid of anybody; we just elevated people into better roles. With the middle managers, a lot of their time was taken up dealing with performance issues with team members, so the middle manager bottlenecks became clearer.

Further, we realized that having a middle manager to manage people's behavior wasn't an efficient use of time. We want people who can manage themselves (and get to work on time), not people who need constant reminders about showing up to their shifts. So we worked on doing a better job at hiring and training. Plus, we adjusted the "middle manager role" to a specialist role, giving them more specific tasks based on their skills and experience. We took time to look at the opportunities, challenges and departmental needs and got really clear on what we needed to work on.

In addition to eliminating middle managers, we keep our teams lean. I want to make an important point. We don't keep our team lean in a way that results in everyone working so hard they become exhausted. A lean team is constantly improving processes to ensure people do their jobs better and more efficiently. Doing the improvement work allows us to maintain a high level of operations without adding people, all while controlling our operating costs even as we get bigger.

An example is our Finance department. They used to add new people into roles as they grew. Instead, we asked: "What technologies can be brought in instead of people? What processes can be improved to streamline everyone's workload?" And it gets people thinking more creatively. You're wasting money and resources if your response to increased work is to keep adding people.

Self-led leaders can't have the autonomy and authority they need if they have to navigate layers of management in order to get a decision made.

Keeping Roles Fluid

Whenever we have a job opening, we do what most companies do: We create a job posting and look for someone who has the skills and experience to fit the job that needs to be done. Obviously those skills are important and we want people who are filling a need. And, as I wrote earlier, it's equally (if not more) important that they are a good culture fit, so that we know they are aligned with our goals and purpose as an organization. It's important to go even further than that.

While we may hire someone for a particular role, we are fluid in our approach. Ultimately, in their journey with us, we want to figure out their skills and gifts and see where they can best thrive. Basically, we're a strengths-based organization. We put people in roles where they feel strong and get to produce great results. That means we have fluidity when it comes to moving and changing roles and enabling people to take on different portfolios. It's part of our culture, and we find it wonderful and exciting.

I spend about 80 percent of my time focused on people's skills and gifts: mentoring self-led leaders, leveraging their skills and encouraging them to pursue the things they're passionate about. (I get more into mentorship in the last chapter.) For instance, our leadership team members are dynamic and diverse in their own skill sets. So as a leader, ask yourself: *How can I leverage everyone's skills? How do I understand what drives them? What gives someone energy? What is their gift? What are they most awesome at?*

I remember doing some training a while back with a team member, and one of our conversations was about when the person was in their place of soulfulness. She said that hers is when she has freedom. And up until that point, her role at Nurse Next Door had morphed into the opposite of that: A lot of people were reporting to her, and she had limited time and freedom to innovate, create and develop new ideas. So I said, "Let's work on that." We had another team member come in and take over some of her responsibilities, which provided her with the space to get creative and thrive again in her role. Now she's doing wonderfully because she has more freedom.

Here's another example. A while back, the team member who did our analytics was doing a fine job. However, you could tell he wasn't energized or excited, and he had a desire to do far more. Now, normally his skills fit within an "IT job description," but we don't put people in boxes. We believe that by having fluidity in roles we can best develop people and help them find their strengths. We're not tied to organizational charts or set ways of doing things. So we decided to have him sit in our systems performance team, which dramatically shifted the way his work was structured. It helped him see how data analytics are integral to our franchisees and enabled him to capture information in a whole different way. These new responsibilities completely energized his role and gave us a different perspective on our data.

In a lot of companies, that kind of job fluidity would be a crazy thing to do. Being able to shift roles—being agile and fluid and not being afraid of change—has actually moved the organization forward because it's helped us find efficiencies faster. It's about making sure people see the meaning behind what they're doing. It's about believing in someone and saying, "Okay, this doesn't work, so let's try something else."

BEING OPEN TO CHANGE

Occasionally someone will say to us, "Wow, you're always changing. People seem to be moving around a lot within the organization." They make this sound like a bad thing. Our response? "Yes, isn't that great!" Our fluidity can be perceived as a weakness. It's actually very intentional and we view it as a strength. We are a people development company. When we see an opportunity that will stretch and grow someone, we provide them with that opportunity. When we allow ourselves to have the space and creativity to be adaptable within our team, we achieve amazing results.

This role fluidity is not about asking someone to fit into the mold of what we think they should be. It's about aligning our company to the person and vice versa. We have to be constantly looking at whether people are thriving. If they're not, we have to figure out why.

We also believe in creating careers. We have many examples of people who have grown within the organization. Our Director, People & Culture, for instance, has been with us over a decade. She began in the Care Services Center and got the exposure she needed to be sitting at the leadership level. We have another person who started by doing intakes and is now Franchise Development Manager. And our Director of Finance started with us in the Finance department of our Vancouver corporate franchise. These types of examples are commonplace. Part of the reason we've been able to be lean is because we determine who in the organization wants to work on their strengths, develop new skills and help push themselves—and the business—forward.

Working as One Team

While self-led leadership and fluid, streamlined teams are important, it's also absolutely essential that everyone in the organization work as One Team and not in silos. Why? Because if people operate in too much of an autonomous fashion, they work in isolation and don't coordinate with other team members to address an opportunity or solve the root cause of an issue. The better our people are as a team, the more they accomplish together.

Silos kill companies because they defer responsibility. When we are united in mind and purpose, we can achieve much more than when we are apart. That's why it's so important to work as One Team that is constantly evolving, where each team member is responsible for contributing to our company goals and generative culture.

So how do you ensure you work as One Team? First off, you need to create ways for your organization to connect and engage with one another. I'll give you some examples of what we do at Nurse Next Door on a regular basis to promote engagement and One Team:

- **Daily huddles:** Every morning we hold a seven-minute daily huddle. At the huddle, we update everyone on our goals (more on that later) and celebrate their results and achievements. Through our Heart Star program, we nominate people who have gone above and beyond to do something truly outstanding, live our core values and make lives better. In addition, we hand out Flowerbucks (our internal "currency") when someone on our team has gone above and beyond in their role. Flowerbucks are also given out to people who have received Heart Star nominations, as well as those who have done the nominating. Ask yourself: *What small activities can I do that bring team members together to review results and celebrate their accomplishments?*

- **The right people in the room:** When we're working on a project or going into a meeting, we ask ourselves: *Do* *we have all the right people here?* For instance, IT used to be siloed from so much of what we did, although their knowledge is instrumental to many of our projects. We now involve them more in meetings and projects as needed to make sure we tap into their expertise. When you think about your own team, make sure you have the right people in meetings so you can produce amazing results. (And while you're at it, open up a meeting invitation to anyone on the team. Sometimes an outside perspective—from someone who's not an "expert" in that area—can bring a much-needed idea or point of view to the table.)

- **Quarterly business reviews:** We host a quarterly business review to go over each department's Bold Goals, results, learnings and challenges, as well as their focus areas for the next quarter. This provides so much insight for the entire organization, as it helps us learn, get curious and understand what people are working on. Regular updates are particularly helpful for making sure you are aligned on culture and goals.

Paying People Well

To ensure their company is successful, many businesses have a lean business model; as a result, people are not always well compensated. The common approach can be to hire junior people and pay them a nominal salary. They may help that person develop their skill set, but it can be hard for team members to increase their pay accordingly. Salaries are one of the biggest parts of a company's overhead, so it makes sense that you'd want to keep salaries as low as you can. Keeping salaries low is a common mindset that should be challenged.

Here's why. I believe the only way you get to profits and success is by paying people extremely well and making sure they feel great about what they're making. Now, there's more to it than that, so bear with me.

We can't just bump up everyone's salaries and call it a day. Instead, we are not stuck on "salary bans." We follow a fluid approach in which we pay people what they're worth and do the right thing.

Paying people well works in conjunction with the rest of our approach: having self-led leaders and eliminating middle management. When we have a lean team of self-led leaders, we have more money to bring in better people and to pay our talented people what they deserve. One exceptional team member will get the work done because they are engaged and excited about what they are doing. We have lean teams in order to get more done and avoid waste.

Here's an example. When I started, there was someone who had been here a long time, and their salary didn't reflect the contribution they were making. So we changed that. And it made a serious difference in their life. It provided a sense of pride and accomplishment. So yes, you could say we took a chance on them. We couldn't afford not to. That person is an amazing leader and has been instrumental in moving our company forward.

We have the same attitude about junior team members. We pay people top of the market for their role even if they're young and inexperienced. We don't take advantage of people. If someone's young and they've been promoted, let's pay them well and develop them into that role, instead of saying, "Well, you don't have the skills yet, so we're not going to pay you for that." If we're not paying them well, it implies that we're saying we don't think they can do the job or develop into it.

Over the years, we have tripled our financial growth and kept our head count low by finding innovation and efficiencies and by focusing on people development. In other words, when our company grew, we didn't automatically hire more people. We balanced strategic hiring with a strong focus on developing the skills and competencies of existing team members. By following this approach, we have self-led people who take responsibility for their roles and drive results.

We also have high expectations around productivity and performance. For instance, we have someone in marketing who is creating amazing results. So why not pay them really well for doing the job versus having two people doing mediocre work?

We also review compensation throughout the year to pay top of market so that team members are well taken care of for the contribution they make.

And by the way, it's not a free ride. If it's not working with someone and we know they're getting paid a lot and not producing, we move on it really fast. We don't do handouts. We have big expectations of people.

An Environment of Fun

We have to enjoy what we're doing. A lean team of self-led leaders will never thrive in an environment that's not enjoyable! That's what inspires them to be innovative and creative. When we create an environment like that, people have the energy and excitement that pops them out of bed in the morning and makes them want to come to work. And that might sound simplistic, but I think we complicate it too often. We thrive when we're having fun and have room to spread our wings. We thrive when we feel like we can do things we didn't know we could do. And our job as leaders is to create the space for people to do that.

When we are young, play is one of the most important things we can do to learn, grow and develop. It's important to be silly, get creative and laugh. Play and fun is also important at work. If we are not having fun or enjoying what we do, then perhaps we shouldn't be doing it.

There's a traditional business mindset that unless we are busy and have a full calendar, we're not being productive. And that if we're having fun, we're not working hard enough. The exact opposite is true. Not only is fun good for the soul, it's also good for engagement and productivity. When there's laughter in the office, that goes a long way.

By fun, it's not just about having parties and outings, though those are great, too. It's about creating a culture of fun and energy and being challenging and excited about projects. So when someone is updating me on what they're doing, I might ask them, "Is it fun? Does it excite you?" Because if they're not having fun and being fulfilled, I want to know why. We try to permeate that culture throughout every interaction and encourage people to go after what they are learning and loving.

It's about having fun finding solutions or working on a project in an area that challenges us. It's about working across departments and with folks we don't normally get to interact with on an everyday basis and creating mentally stimulating environments. We challenge ourselves to find fun in as many areas as possible.

We also like to reward people for their accomplishments. Every quarter, we hold an All-Star Party to acknowledge the person who has contributed the most to Making Lives Better during that period. At these parties, we have lots of perks, like using Flowerbucks to bid on prizes such as gift cards for restaurants or hotel stays, or classes in rock climbing, snowshoeing or yoga. The thing is, we do it because it's really fun. One of our team members makes a great emcee and we are literally laughing the entire time. It's like going to recess; people are just comfortable being able to have fun and be themselves.

Generating an Abundance Mindset

If you are not used to coming from a place of abundance, it can take time to shift. It really is a mindset. It's often as simple as paying attention to your thought patterns and noticing when you are coming from a place of scarcity, not abundance, then shifting your narrative. You may notice you are viewing something as a problem, and when you shift the narrative, you realize you can view it as an opportunity. When you do that, possibilities open up so much more.

BOLD KIND REFLECTIONS: ABUNDANCE MINDSET

- What does Continuous Improvement look like to you?
- How do the people you work with inspire you and lift you up?
- How can you make the shift from a Scarcity Mindset to an Abundance Mindset?
- In what ways can you and your team do better?

CHAPTER 10

REAL CONVERSATIONS

I remember a few years ago having a difficult conversation with a member of the team. I provided feedback that was intended to support them and help them improve; it was not a personal attack. However, this individual didn't see it that way at first and felt that I was criticizing their skills and performance. They left my office feeling frustrated and were focused on what had gone wrong in the past instead of focusing on how to improve in the future.

Over the next few days, we talked about it some more. We really dove into the conversation, and I took the time to understand why the person perceived it the way they did. It opened up a dialogue in which I was curious to get their perspective. I did that because I cared about that person. While I wasn't thrilled with their reaction to the initial conversation, I continued to invest time into the conversation and worked to develop the relationship and this individual. Ultimately they started to recognize that my feedback came from me wanting to help them grow personally and professionally. The experience showed me something important. We're so used to being on the defensive in a workplace and not directly saying what we mean that when we actually communicate from an honest and caring viewpoint, it can throw people off.

This type of defensive behavior is not uncommon. It's fairly routine to see people in corporate America show up to work with their guard up. Many people haven't had great experiences with their workplaces or their leaders. People show up late, aren't engaged, complain about their bosses or contribute to negative work environments. There's a strong emphasis on people showing up to work as a victim in a toxic work culture. This has been allowed and even expected. It's just the way things are.

In response, the company's Human Resources department is often brought in and expected to defuse some of those problems or "manage" that person. HR puts on a Band-Aid to create a solution for the fact that there are deep-rooted issues around expectations and how people show up at work. In a lot of traditional organizations, people are set up to be told what to do and tick off their list of tasks/responsibilities. People can't have or are not expected to have real conversations or provide genuine feedback. And I think people see it is detrimental, and they don't know what to do about it.

And hey, I get it. It's hard to give and receive feedback. It's hard to have real conversations. It takes fortitude, skill, patience and compassion. It can be uncomfortable to be in a real conversation where stakes may be high and you need to say what needs to be said.

Luckily, however, that's been changing more and more.

Many companies are leading the charge in innovative workplace practices, and people have become less willing to put up with toxic workplace cultures. That's become even more evident since COVID. People had the chance to pause their work lives and reassess what they really want. A lot of them don't want to go back to the way things were. They don't want to settle. They want humanity. They want to bring their whole selves to work and be respected for who they are.

That means that now, more than ever, it's essential to have a workplace environment where we are intentional about our actions and are able to have bold, important and real conversations. I believe we need to have workplaces in which we genuinely care. Why? Because it's all one life, whether it's work or home. And we are people with stories, friends and families. We can't separate out different parts of it; it's not natural.

As home care providers, Nurse Next Door caregivers have firsthand experience in having bold, real conversations with families who are dealing with health issues, as well as mortality. While your business is probably not facing the same life-and-death situations, I'm willing to bet there are still important conversations to be had. Problems in our personal lives inevitably affect our work lives. There's the team member whose mother has died, and they are struggling with depression. Someone may be having financial difficulties or going through divorce. Or there may be someone who is unhappy with the trajectory of their life and not doing their best work. We're all people, and we all experience both joy and suffering. We all have periods when we excel and when we are struggling.

People want to be respected, cared for and listened to. And when we take the time to do that, to genuinely reach out to someone, that's when everything opens up. By caring for our teams and having honest and open conversations with them, they feel seen and heard. They feel they *matter*. They're more excited about pursuing things in life that are important to them, and they're more apt to value their relationship with us. Because it *is* a relationship we are having with our team members. It's up to us to make that relationship matter.

This is where REAL Conversations come in. REAL Conversations are about having open, honest and caring dialogue with team members. This concept was originally inspired by Kim Scott's Radical Candor—caring personally and challenging directly—as a way of providing feedback and having hard conversations.

However, REAL Conversations go far beyond providing feedback. REAL Conversations are about showing up as our full selves and caring meaningfully about the other person in every interaction we have with them. These aren't one-way conversations; they're about both people being willing, present participants, with an open, two-way dialogue. In REAL Conversations, we have a meaningful relationship with someone, free of ego or blame. We come from a place of abundance and possibility, and we aren't afraid to lean in and really listen to what they are saying.

When I think about how REAL Conversations started at Nurse Next Door, I go back to a meeting I had with the leadership team some years back. I remember asking a challenging question about a difficult topic. To be fair, it was a hard question to answer, and the conversation quickly shifted to something else. Nobody wanted to address this difficult topic. After a little while, I circled back to it and said we needed to talk about it. I couldn't leave it alone. And I'm so glad we addressed it. It opened up a whole conversation about the topic. We also talked openly about how we needed to do a better job of leaning in and having the conversation, even if it's uncomfortable. We shouldn't walk by what's happening.

We also realized we were having too many conversations about the same thing. Someone would bring up an issue in a meeting, and it wouldn't get fully discussed. We'd acknowledge it and dabble in the topic but wouldn't own the conversation and fully address it. So we'd leave the meeting and it would come up again in *another* meeting. And sometimes even *another* meeting. I believe that if something needs to be said, it should be said directly, the first time. We have to go *through* it, not *around* it. All of the above were catalysts to making a commitment as a team that we would have the REAL Conversation in the *first* conversation.

Like anything, when you first start creating a new habit or trying a new approach, there is always learning. This is the great thing about trying something new; there is so much room for growth and evolution. When we first made the commitment to have REAL Conversations, it didn't always go very well. We learned that some conversations work better in a public forum and some are best kept private. We also initially struggled with the bold aspect of REAL Conversations. Sometimes we may have *thought* we were being caring. Instead, we may have been too direct or jumped into the conversation without first connecting with them personally.

We realized that the secret sauce at Nurse Next Door is not only about being bold, it's also about amplifying the care. We cannot have a REAL Conversation unless we come from a place of genuine care and are in a meaningful relationship with the person we are talking to. That's why I love having conversations on my couch; it's the perfect setting for both of us to be genuine and real and to have a conversation on equal footing. While I recognize not everyone may have a couch in their office, I encourage leaders to find a space that creates a humanized setting to engage in real conversations.

Now that I have talked about the what and the why, let's get into the *how*.

How to Have REAL Conversations

REAL Conversations don't just *happen*. They take skill and practice. To make REAL Conversations work, we have to genuinely care about the well-being of our team members, be interested in their lives and want them to succeed. After taking our learnings about what has worked and not worked over the years, we evolved our approach. For us, the secret sauce to having a REAL conversation consists of four key components:

- R: Having a meaningful Relationship with the individual and creating trust to speak openly and honestly
- E: Being Egoless and letting go of self-importance

- A: Coming from a place of Abundance and having an open, curious attitude

- L: Being able to Lean into the discomfort of having a hard conversation

Let's get into each of them now.

R: A meaningful relationship

A meaningful relationship is one that's based on trust, care and mutual respect. It's about feeling safe and comfortable enough to be yourself around the other person. You can have a meaningful relationship with someone you've only known a short while, and even with someone with whom you have little in common, as long as you genuinely care about their well-being and value them.

I believe you can only have a REAL Conversation—one that is truly honest, real and vulnerable—when you are in a meaningful relationship. It is the foundation of everything. Here's an example of why that is. When I first started having REAL Conversations, I found that I sometimes went into situations with an assumption that I had a mutually caring and trustful relationship with the other person, and we could be candid and open with one another. In other words, I may have thought there was a level of confidence and trust that hadn't yet been established by *both* of us.

I've since learned that I can't practice Bold Kindness and have a REAL Conversation without building that relationship first. The trust won't be there. Think of the best relationships in your life. Trust, care and respect are typically at the forefront. You may not always agree with each other, but you trust and respect each other, and you can easily move past those differences. So if I'm not sure if the relationship is there, I work on it. I spend more time getting to know someone—and helping them get to know me—until we build up trust and rapport.

It's important to consistently cultivate a relationship with someone, whether we've just met them or have known them for a long time. How are we showing that we care personally? Do we give them our full attention and look them in the eye when we're talking to them? Do we know what's important to them? Do they have dreams and goals? Every conversation is an opportunity to get to know someone more intimately.

Every interaction with a team member should focus on *both* personal and business. For instance, when we go into meetings, we don't just head right into the business at hand. We always start by asking someone about their day or their weekend or what they've been up to. We ask questions. We get curious about who they are and what matters to them. And sometimes we chat about personal stuff, and sometimes it takes much longer. What matters is that we are, first and foremost, showing a genuine interest in the other person and making it clear that their lives are important to us.

Even if there's an issue, we continue to approach it with curiosity. For instance, if somebody didn't do a great job on something, we don't scold them, blame them or call them out. We approach it with care and empathy and ask them what happened, what went wrong and if everything is okay. We ask them what they learned and what they will do differently next time. Every mistake or miss is an opportunity for growth.

This isn't about making a team member your new best friend. If they're not someone you would want to have over for dinner, that's okay. They still deserve respect. They deserve to have someone care about them and be curious about who they are and what they are thinking. If we don't genuinely care about our team members, they will sense it. And they won't trust us, be honest with us or fully open up to our feedback without taking it personally.

E: An egoless self

REAL Conversations require both parties to be egoless: to remove arrogance and self-importance from the conversation. They require a willingness to listen, learn, grow and be coachable.

When team members come to the table with an egocentric attitude, something's up. We tend to behave like that when we are feeling defensive or insecure or we don't trust the person we're talking to. So again, to help counter that, we have to build the relationship first. We have to let them know we care. When we show care and compassion to others, they're more likely to let their guard down and have a sense of trust and openhearted-ness. They are more likely to understand the feedback is rooted in learning and Continuous Improvement and to take that feed-back and feel great about it.

However, it goes beyond compassion and care. We need to create space for team members to be coached in these situations and feel like they matter.

It's one of the reasons why it's so important to have self-led leaders in an organization. Self-led leaders are open to feedback, being coached and discovering a new way. And if they're not open to feedback or Continuous Improvement, they're probably not self-led leaders and they're probably not right for our organization. And that's okay.

Likewise, team leaders need to be open and egoless. (I address this more in the chapter on mentoring.) In traditional organizations, it's very easy for leaders to feel like they're the most important people at the table. They're not. Our team members are. We have to remind ourselves that we don't have all the answers and that our team needs to help us along the way. We need our team so that our organization can grow.

When I first joined Nurse Next Door, the cofounders had already created an incredible brand with a strong core purpose of Making Lives Better. I wanted to make sure we maintained the culture that the owners had worked so hard to build, while at the same time expanding the business and improving financial performance. I also knew that to expand the company further, I needed to make changes to the leadership team. I needed the right people to work on the right things, so we could scale the business. And it was incredibly important to me that the team adapt to these new changes and continue to thrive.

I quickly learned that I needed to create an open dialogue with the team to establish trust and enable change. So I let go of my ego and asked for feedback at all levels. I told them what I was doing and encouraged people to contribute. Instead of just implementing new initiatives that I thought were best, I had conversations around each one. I was open to having my point of view be shifted.

Even when I'm not implementing a new initiative, I am consistently ensuring I have an open dialogue with my team. This can be done through weekly updates or one-on-ones; it's whatever works best for you. My office door is always open, and when someone wants to chat, we sit on the couch and have a conversation. I always spend a portion of the day just walking around the office, talking to people and seeing what they're up to. I feel like this results in real, authentic relationships that aren't built on hierarchy or ego.

A: A place of abundance

REAL Conversations need to come from a place of abundance. They require us to suspend judgment and be genuinely open to possibilities. To hold off on having the answers and be curious about what else is out there. To be willing to listen and learn.

Listening is key to that. In chapter 5, I talk about the need for leaders to listen to themselves. It's also important to apply that skill to listening to all of our team. Listening is one of the hardest things to do and one of the most crucial. So I spend a lot of time creating white space to bring quiet in. It's about cultivating self-awareness: listening to myself, noticing my own thoughts and patterns, then shifting them. I must first do the internal work on myself before I can listen to others and be fully present.

If I don't agree with them, I don't tell them I think they're wrong. I just ask more questions. I want to understand what they're passionate about and why they feel that way.

When you go into a conversation, take a minute to check in with yourself, to see where your mindset is at. Do you feel open and curious about interacting with this person? Do you feel like you can be fully present? And maybe you're not. It happens. Sometimes we're in a conversation and not giving it 100 percent. If I'm distracted and not completely engaged in providing full feedback, it doesn't go well. So then I look back and think: *How can I do better? What can I learn? How can I come from a place of abundance?*

If you recognize that you're not fully participating in a conversation that is important, it's okay. We're human. Let it go. Reschedule it for another time. Or at least go back to that person and have the conversation again, with full presence and intent this time.

L: Leaning into discomfort

Finally, REAL Conversations are about leaning into the discomfort of having a hard conversation. And let's face it: some conversations are hard. Sometimes we have to talk about things that are difficult to discuss. It's so important to lean into the discomfort and to be okay with getting vulnerable.

So much of the time we are feeling nervous about having a conversation with someone and we hold onto stress because of this. Or we're fearful that we've done something wrong or we're going to be judged or blamed. At Nurse Next Door, we're not a culture of blame or judgment. We have to be okay with things being vulnerable and real. In my experience, people are often nervous about being bold and honest in conversations with their peers. They get stressed when they have to have hard and sweaty discussions. Sometimes it is because they don't want to hurt people's feelings or cause "conflict." Or they just don't have the tools or confidence to navigate the conversation.

It's a skill that improves the more we do it. It can be scary to give and receive feedback, but when it's done honestly and with care, it can be transformative.

We also need to lean into the truth. Sometimes things go wrong, and people stay silent. They don't want to look weak. At Nurse Next Door, we try to flag things when we see them and not let something fester. And when something goes wrong, we ask ourselves: *When did we know? What could we have done differently?* By leaning in and approaching it with curiosity, we get much better results.

Real Communication, Real Results

At Nurse Next Door, we have real, hard and sweaty conversations in the moment, every day. It's how we grow. It's how we evolve. It's how we learn and get results. It's how we get work done faster by increasing our workability with one another. "The meeting after the meeting" doesn't work for us. Instead, we have REAL Conversations that are caring and direct, even when people are at their most vulnerable. We talk about hard topics. And we believe the truest, most respectful thing is to have that hard conversation, even when it's sticky and awkward. Otherwise, we're not addressing what people really need, and we're not giving them the respect they deserve.

Trying to reshape a traditional organization into a Bold Kind enterprise requires a lot of communication. You need to talk about challenging areas such as changing expectations, being fluid around roles and showing people they can trust you not to harshly judge their mistakes. Working on REAL Conversations will help you navigate all of these subjects more smoothly.

BOLD KIND REFLECTIONS: REAL CONVERSATIONS

- What do you need to do to develop more trusting and meaningful relationships with your team members?
- How do you quiet your ego?
- When was the last time you had a heart-centered conversation?
- What conversation do you need to have today that you don't want to have?

MENTORING, NOT MANAGING

I n this last chapter, I want to finish off with a core belief and mindset that drives everything we do here at Nurse Next Door: Mentoring, Not Managing. Mentoring is the backbone of a Bold Kind culture: It's how we guide our team members and is key to people development.

Nurse Next Door's team members don't need leaders who manage them and tell them what to do. I believe that when you manage people, you rob them of their development. People need leaders who mentor first: who serve as consultants and advisers and guide and help develop their growth. We provide the *what* (the goal, including the measure of success) and the *why* and challenge them to come up with the *how* (the solution).

Bold Kind mentors don't just offer help or advice. They empower their team to be self-led and to cultivate an Abundance Mindset. Bold Kind mentors support their team in working toward a common purpose and in having REAL Conversations. They get out of the way and let team members shine.

Through mentoring, we also incorporate situational leadership. This isn't a one-size-fits-all approach; we adapt our mentoring approach to the specific person or situation we are in. For instance, someone who is new to Nurse Next Door may need more direction and support when they are taking on a new task.

Most importantly, at Nurse Next Door, Bold Kind mentors *care about* and *believe in* team members. This is an essential part of the equation. That means that we ask lots of questions. We provide the *what* and the *why*, not the *how*. We listen. We help individuals develop their potential to grow and accomplish goals. To truly function as a people development organization, we have to believe in our people and want to develop meaningful relationships with them.

Here's an example of what it means to have leaders who are mentors instead of managers. When a member of the leadership team is meeting with another team member to get updated on a project, they will ask lots of questions about how things are going. At the same time, they won't provide the answers. They won't tell the other person what to do. Instead, they will provide guidance and give them the space to come up with a solution for themselves. We don't lead the meeting. We encourage our team members to create the agenda. When they ask questions, we may respond with, "What do *you* think?"

It might be easier to give someone the answer and be done with the conversation in a few minutes, but in doing so, we're not encouraging that team member to think through possible solutions and feel like they have a seat at the table in leading the decision. Our job as mentors is to create the conditions for growth and potential.

Our leadership team has always emphasized mentoring over managing, and in recent years we have become more intentional about it. And a lot of that is because of COVID. At the very beginning of this book, I talk about COVID and how it completely disrupted the world: Businesses changed overnight and had to find new ways of thriving. People began reevaluating their values and priorities in life and work. Many of them quit their jobs and looked for something better. They began questioning the traditional ways of doing business and decided they wanted something more. There was a fundamental shift in the traditional mindset of how people work.

And at Nurse Next Door, this gave us the opportunity to pause and think about where *we* wanted to go as an organization. We believe we need to be continuously improving and that, as leaders, we can do more and be more. So we asked ourselves: *How can we do better? What's the next evolution of our leadership team, and who do we need to be? How do we grow as a people development organization?*

We know that people want autonomy and choice. They want the ability to make their own decisions without being told what to do. (People don't tend to enjoy being micromanaged.) They want to feel fulfilled in their roles and supported in their journey. So we became even more deliberate about our leadership approach. In a sense, this required more of a shift in mindset than anything else. As leaders, we took a stance to say it is not about us being at the head of the table. It's not about us at all.

It's about us standing by the side, cheering our people on. We need to give them space to shine. So we listen more and talk less. We ask more questions and let them find the answers.

I think it's very similar to being a mom. I learned to give my kids enough space so they can each be their own person. And that is not always easy to do. I admire the approach described in *The Danish Way of Parenting*, which is based on the premise that kids are capable of anything.[5] I don't fix their problems, and I don't make any decisions without an explanation. And I believe this approach works with anybody, not just children.

I try to apply the same attitude to the team. To develop people, we need to show people we care, and we need to empower autonomy to allow them to think, create, design and thrive. If they always rely on me for permission or approval, I won't be able to give them the space to be self-led leaders and grow, learn, develop or make mistakes.

For instance, early on, one of my team members asked for my approval on how to do something in my very first meeting with her. I told her she didn't need my approval and that I didn't want her to ask for it. Instead, I wanted her to bring to the table her thoughts or recommendations on that particular item so we could discuss it and ultimately make the decision together. If I gave her the answers, I wouldn't be leading; I'd be managing. How can this individual learn and grow if I just tell her exactly what to do, instead of having her think for herself?

Let's explore more of what it means to mentor, not manage, at Nurse Next Door.

---

5   For more information, see https://thedanishway.com/.

Bold Kind Mentoring

Mentors guide; they don't direct. They let go of their own agenda. Instead, they seek to fully understand their mentees and support them in their growth. Again, this is a mindset. You need to believe in the importance of this work and to cultivate a culture and environment that enable you to practice this day after day. A change in mindset or behavior doesn't happen overnight. It takes practice, discipline and belief.

At Nurse Next Door, we consistently practice the following steps to help us develop our people through mentorship.

1. Building meaningful relationships

To fully mentor people, we have to be in a meaningful relationship with them. That means trusting each other and feeling comfortable about talking about things that matter. When we have a meaningful relationship with our team members, they take chances. They speak their truth. They reach out to us for support.

To do that, we need to understand and be interested in our team members. If we're not interested in our people—what they are doing and where they are going—they are not going to grow and excel in their lives and work.

In an earlier chapter, I talk about how we don't save up meaningful conversations for annual reviews. Instead, *we have those conversations every day.* Conversations about performance and growth should not be saved up for annual reviews. Instead, we develop people on a regular, consistent basis.

I strongly believe in taking the time to get to know people on our team. That could mean going for a walk or grabbing a coffee together, holding quarterly team building events or making time to express genuine gratitude to team members.

Here's where curiosity (an important theme in this book) comes in handy. I ask questions to learn about someone's life and what makes them happy. I talk to my team and ask them: "While you're here, what do you want to accomplish?" I am in conversation with them. I want to give them the space and security to say, "I want to be here for five years," or "I want to be here for six months," and for everyone to be on board with that. When I'm having that honest conversation and respecting what someone wants, I'm providing them with the autonomy to choose their own path.

Being in a meaningful relationship means that we care for their whole selves, not just who they are at work. For instance, we love helping teams find outside jobs or start their own businesses. I know that sounds counterintuitive, and it can take a while for people to believe in and trust that. Ultimately, we have everyone's best interests at heart. As a result, they're more likely to maximize the time they're with us and make a great contribution, rather than just go through the motions.

2. Providing the what and why, not the how

We don't tell people how to do something. We provide team members with the *what* (what we want the business to achieve) and the *why* (why the business needs to achieve this) then let them figure out the *how*. We set the stage, then we *get out of the way*.

Our team needs to understand our strategy. If they don't know what we want to achieve and why we are doing something, they won't be set up for success because they won't have a clear picture of the goal and how their actions contribute to the bigger picture.

This has been a key strategy in how I mentor my team when it comes to decision-making. For example, I recall at one point someone wanted to implement a change to how we work. I could see it would have a negative impact on Nurse Next Door's culture and go against who we are. While it seemed like such a small change to that individual, the ripple effect would actually dramatically affect how we worked.

We needed to talk through it so they could see the bigger picture. We sat down on my couch and discussed *what* we wanted to achieve and *why* we were doing it. At the end of our talk, they saw that their proposed change—their *how*—didn't align with our goal or with who we are as an organization. So they came up with another option.

At Nurse Next Door, we are very transparent about communicating our financial and business goals. Every day, team members can clearly see the results displayed on our systems and dashboard. This includes our daily, weekly and monthly goals for revenue, intakes and sales. We clearly communicate this information because we know our people are the ones who are driving those results.

Once they have the what and why, team members are asked to figure out the solution. And how do we help them do that? We literally get out of the way. As leaders, we are very intentional about which meetings we attend. Our team doesn't need us at the table, dictating what they should do. We let them figure out what to do. We give them space to have autonomy and do their jobs.

When we do meet with team members to discuss their progress, we get curious. We ask questions and let them come up with the answers. Then we ask more questions. Now, as part of having that conversation, I might throw out a bunch of ideas or thoughts that occur to me. That doesn't mean I expect team members to implement those ideas. I would hope they consider my input, then do what they think is best. (See the section below on letting go of our egos—this is a key element in letting team members do their own thing.)

It does take practice to break old patterns of behavior in which we, as leaders, dictate the way things should be done. For instance, a team member may come to me with an idea, and my immediate thought might be: *This isn't going to work.* After all, I have years of experience, and I may have unsuccessfully tried to implement the same idea at another time. The thing is, sometimes I'm wrong! I constantly practice pausing and letting the individual talk through the idea or opportunity, then give them the space they need to further investigate it or come up with a solution. And I'm often pleasantly surprised to see that they come at the idea with an approach I hadn't thought of, and it works wonderfully. I think it's important to remind ourselves that we, as leaders, can get stuck in our own ways and ideas. We need to be continuously changing and challenging our own approaches.

Earlier in this book, I also talk about allowing and encouraging mistakes. That's an incredibly important part of mentorship. If mistakes are made or things didn't go the way they expected, we don't judge. We get curious. "How did it go? What did you learn? What would you do differently next time?" We encourage people to look at opportunities and find solutions.

There is one other important step here: establishing clear methods of communication. In other words, it's imperative that we provide guidance on how our team should communicate with us as mentors. For instance, I might formalize the best method and frequency for giving me updates (e.g., weekly check-ins) and when they should seek my advice. (Of course, as I talk about earlier, I also have an open-door policy, so people can feel free to pop in at any time if they want to chat about something.) If these boundaries aren't clear, there may be collateral damage: People might make decisions without fully understanding the ripple effects. By providing the goal, getting out of the way and touching base as needed, we can help our teams be self-led leaders who come up with amazing results.

3. Removing fear and cultivating confidence

In chapter 6 I talk about how important it is to not let fear and lack of confidence stop us from following our instincts as leaders. The same is true for our team members.

Fear is a very real part of life and a natural part of being a human being. It's a big reason why people may not strive to do more or worry about making mistakes. A key part of a mentor's role is to talk about a team member's fears and level of confidence and uncover the truths and misperceptions. It's our job to help build up confidence in people and empower them to proceed, despite their trepidation.

When we do big things, it's scary. And being a self-led leader can be scary. We all have to ask ourselves: *Am I willing to take risks? Am I willing to make mistakes?* It takes courage and confidence to be self-led, and those qualities don't come naturally to everyone.

So how do we create that possibility and give people the confidence that they can make mistakes and innovate without being afraid of "consequences"? That they can have whatever they want?

We do it by leading with our hearts and by being human and real. To create confidence, we start by welcoming someone's true self and allowing them to shine. Our team members gain confidence when their contributions are welcome, and they see they are an important part of our organization. When they have that internal confidence and don't need external reassurance, no one is self-absorbed or stuck on themselves.

We had a team member once who excelled in her work. Her challenge was that she was very nervous about making presentations in front of a group of people. So we supported her in developing the skills and confidence she needed to speak publicly. We encouraged her to do small, one-on-one presentations first, slowly moving to a larger group. We also provided the opportunity for her to take a public speaking course if she wanted to. An important aspect of mentorship was giving her the guidance and feedback along the way to help her gain those skills.

We also set the expectation that we accept and welcome mistakes. Making mistakes means we are trying something new and thinking differently. So we check in with team members early on. When we are about to embark on a bold new project, we ask people, "How do you feel about it?" If they're uncertain or scared, we want to know. We help them navigate the path of where they need to go. We're not afraid to be vulnerable, to be in the REAL Conversation or to support each other.

I like to think of it as creating moments of learning. How do we help someone get better, without coming from a place of judgment? So much of business has been about judgment. Instead, we need to think about it like this: *You're already great, and how can I help you be even better?*

I go back to being a parent. How does a parent build confidence in their kids? How does a parent encourage and teach their children? Should the parent just tell their kid what to do? Or should they get into a conversation with them? Let's make sure we have the conversation. Let's help people feel listened to and respected so their confidence soars.

4. Letting go of ego

Throughout this book, I talk a lot about how important it is to be our full selves: to be honest and vulnerable about who we are. And that includes letting go of our egos.

To be good mentors, we have to make sure we're not letting ourselves get in the way of our team members' growth. The thing is, it's really not about us. We're not the star of the show; our team members are. They're the ones who are making it happen; we're just supporting them along the way.

Leaders have to let go of their own egos and let others shine. This isn't always as easy to do as we might think. There are some leaders who seem to always want to prove they are the best, that they know more than others or that they have power and authority over their team. They put their self-interests ahead of the feelings and needs of others. They operate from a place where ego rules.

It's impossible to mentor others if we come from a place of ego. It's not the route of leadership. If we come from a place of ego, it's impossible for team members to be fully engaged and come to work each day and for them to excel in their jobs. People whose egos are driving their decisions are not focused on developing others or creating a culture where people thrive.

When I think about ego, I go back to Respect, a principle of Happier Aging. It means we show care, concern and consideration for others, even when they're different from us. Ego can stand in the way of respect. We need our leaders to challenge themselves to think about how they can ensure their team members step into their confidence.

The role of a mentor is to help their team members shine without taking the credit for themselves. It's about being able to take the company to a new level. We must ensure our leaders are mentors who believe in developing other people and who are willing to let go of control and replace their egos with trust in other team members.

In short, moving from leadership to mentorship is another

form of risk-taking. If leaders aren't taking chances on their teams, they're not learning and doing their job.

5. Encouraging people to pursue their dreams

Earlier in the book I talk about how we have a Bold Dreams Bold Goals program in which we support our team members in determining their dreams and goals and putting plans in place to achieve them. As mentors, one of the very best things we can do is support them in their dreams and goals, whether those involve staying at the organization or even leaving it.

When COVID came around, many people had the opportunity to stop and think about what they really want—what their dreams and goals are—and many people decided to go for it. We had several people come forward and say, "I've always wanted to start my own company and now is the time." I love that. It's so amazing that we've helped someone get there. They're going to go off and start a new company or pursue something they love, partially because they learned so much here and had the time to do it. I love that we've been on the journey with them, in whatever way we were able to help. How can we help support people to go on to the next thing? So that really is how the conversation can go, if we're in the right place of talking about what people truly love doing.

We also have to support the fact that our business won't always work for everyone. For instance, as we continue to make changes in business, there are going to be people who are not on board. It's inevitable. There are people who love to be part of an exciting growth mindset and there are people who don't. And the people who started the business with us, and grew it to where it is, might not be the ones to grow it to the next level.

People pursue dreams that take them away from Nurse Next Door. Others leave because the changes we're making don't work for them. We think that's okay. It's about celebrating what everyone brings to the table as they go on a growth journey with the organization. If someone sees something in their future or career path, we want to learn about it. We want to explore it and encourage it. Sometimes it means they expand their skill set, which supports the business, and other times it might mean they pursue something outside of Nurse Next Door. How awesome is it that we get to be part of that journey and be really proud to support them on their path to happiness and growth? It's an amazing way we get to contribute to the business community. It just gets me so excited!

Empowering Ourselves— and Our Teams

Mentoring people—truly caring about someone as an individual and empowering them to chart their own course—is one of the most challenging things a leader can do. It means we have to approach a relationship without ego and stop telling people what to do, even if we know the answer. *Especially* if we know the answer. For us at Nurse Next Door, it's an ongoing learning process, one that will never stop.

When we succeed as mentors, we not only help our team

members, but we also help ourselves. We see where our challenges are and what to pay attention to. We learn how we respond to certain situations and how to improve. And when we can approach this process with an openhearted attitude, we truly bring Bold Kindness to everyone.

Really, when it comes down to it, Bold Kindness is about helping us all be our truest, most authentic selves, pursue our hopes and dreams and make our own mark on this world. Supporting each other on this journey is one of the most valuable things we can do as human beings.

BOLD KIND REFLECTIONS:
MENTORING, NOT MANAGING

- Where can you let go of control?
- Why would people want to be mentored by you?
- How do you support your team to dream?
- What are three things you can do today to mentor more and manage less?

BOLD KINDNESS
NEVER STOPS

When I look back on how we've evolved as an organization, I am so proud of how far we've come. I'm also curious. What's next? How do we stay in the mindset of Continuous Improvement and keep developing ourselves personally and professionally?

Our next steps are to continue to stay bold. To continue challenging and disrupting our market while staying true to our purpose of Making Lives Better. We also know that what got us here is not what's going to get us to the next level. So we're never done.

We've already impacted lives through Happier Aging. We will continue to expand our efforts so more people have Choice, Autonomy, Respect, Purpose and Belonging in their lives and are able to live well until the very end. We are also in the midst of a huge initiative called Caregiving as a Career in which we are transforming the home care industry and ensuring caregivers are paid competitively and provided with growth and development opportunities.

And my head goes to even bigger possibilities, possibilities that affect all of us. How can we, as mentors, do a better job of coming together to create kind, compassionate businesses where people love coming to work? How can we inspire each other and bring creativity and joy into the workplace? How can we learn from and share with each other?

Adopting Bold Kindness is very rewarding because it encourages people to fully express themselves and live one full life. In doing so, we are able to thrive and care for ourselves and others, embrace self-led leadership and approach our lives from a perspective of abundance, not scarcity. Through Bold Kindness, we can help ourselves, and our companies, grow.

I hope you will start challenging yourself and your organization to explore Bold Kindness. How can you get into REAL Conversations and cultivate a culture of Continuous Improvement with people who aren't afraid to take risks? How can you get out of the way and mentor instead of manage? How can you challenge your own mindset, and your team members, to transform into a Bold Kind team that boldly leads your company into its next evolution?

I'll admit this kind of change is not an easy journey. Culture shifts take time. Mistakes will be made. We have to be okay with that. We have to be okay with being vulnerable and with being honest about how we can do better. We have to be brave enough to move away from hierarchical, ego-driven infrastructures that don't serve us.

The best way to start? By beginning a conversation about Bold Kindness with your colleagues, your team members and your friends. Let them know you're just starting this journey yourself. Be curious about the possibilities. They're always out there, even if we don't see them yet. We have an opportunity to transform business as we know it, and it starts with *us*.

Let's keep the conversation going.

ACKNOWLEDGMENTS

This book would not be possible without my amazing team at Nurse Next Door. I am so grateful to all of you for joining me on this Bold Kind journey and for challenging and supporting me along the way. To Ken Sim, owner of Nurse Next Door, thank you for believing in me, giving me the freedom to continue to disrupt the home care industry and supporting us in our quest of Making Lives Better. And, most importantly, to my children, Jackson and Sophia. You were both my inspiration for Bold Kindness, helping me to embrace and challenge people development and create a kinder, more authentic workplace and future for you both.

ABOUT ME

HI, I'M CATHY.

I am a mother, a daughter, a friend and a mentor.

People have suggested that this section should include my professional achievements, awards and accolades. And that it should tell you why I'm qualified to speak about a concept called Bold Kindness. Here are the most important things I think you should know about me.

I am driven by something I deeply believe in: people.

I believe every person has the potential to achieve great things. I am passionate about people development, and I believe that by empowering others to achieve their dreams, we can help them create lives they love.

As a child, I loved helping my friends and classmates succeed. As I grew older, that passion evolved into a career in leadership, where I've been able to support and mentor countless individuals in their professional journeys. Before I joined Nurse Next Door (a global home care franchise company) as President & CEO, I spent over fifteen years with a Fortune 500 clothing retailer, where I was ultimately responsible for expanding their presence in Germany. I was also President of a Canadian children's retailer before starting my own consulting business, where I helped companies expand their leadership, operational excellence and governance practices.

Throughout my journey, the concept of an Abundance Mindset has been particularly transformative for me. When I come from a place where anything is possible and look to the future, I believe we can create change for the better. This mindset solidified when I became a mom. I knew that I wanted more for my children and their generation (and the next generation and the next). Leading with an Abundance Mindset shifted so much for me on a personal level. On a business level, it has produced some remarkable results for Nurse Next Door across North America, Australia and most recently England.

I believe that we all can live exceptional lives and that it is time for a movement to change how we do business, and most importantly, how we treat and develop people. I believe that movement starts today with Bold Kindness.